MEETING GOD
BEHIND ENEMY LINES:

MY CHRISTIAN TESTIMONY AS A
U.S. NAVY SEAL

STEVE WATKINS

Meeting God Behind Enemy Lines

For Information:

To order more copies:
www.kresschristianpublications.com

or call:
1-8MOREBOOKS
1-(866)-732-6657
ISBN: 0-9671057-0-6

Printed in the United States of America

TO DAD AND MOM,
TWO MORE GIFTS OF
GOD'S AMAZING GRACE.

CONTENTS

FOREWORD

As a Vietnam combat veteran (I piloted an Air Cushion Vehicle in the northern part of South Vietnam and served as operational briefer for then Vice Admiral Zumwalt, Commander Naval Forces Vietnam in Saigon), I can easily identify more than 30 years later with Steve Watkins' military experiences during Desert Shield and Desert Storm in the Middle East. We both had an enthusiastic commitment to serving and protecting our country.

But for Steve and me, the military experience was just the means that God used to point us both to our great need for embracing Jesus Christ as Savior and Lord. We both were saved while in the Navy and quickly discovered that the military style of life was personally incompatible with our new found faith in the Redeemer. Steve colorfully recounts his conversion in this spellbinding testimony.

Although I am old enough to be Steve's dad, I can still remember the thrill of reaching the decision to leave the Navy I loved and enter seminary to serve the Lord I loved even more. Reading of Steve's similar experience rekindled wonderful memories of that dramatic, life transforming transition for me. Our paths first crossed when Steve entered The Master's Seminary where I serve as Dean. I watched firsthand and relived my own seminary days as I saw Steve grow in his faith at TMS. Steve excelled in his studies and has now returned to Kentucky for ministry. We both have been dramatically impacted in ministry by the militarylike exhortation, "Suffer hardship with me as a good soldier of Christ

"ONWARD CHRISTIAN SOLDIERS"

Jesus. No soldier in active service entangles himself in the affairs of everyday life, so that he may please the One who enlisted him as a soldier (2 Timothy 2:3-4)."

You will be greatly encouraged to read about Steve's pilgrimage from his patriotism in the military to pursuing the ministry. He has redirected all of his capabilities and courage away from serving his country's temporal needs to serving the eternal purposes of his God.

RICHARD MAYHUE, TH.D.
The Master's Seminary
Sun Valley, California

ACKNOWLEDGEMENTS
~~PREFACE~~

I am grateful to the individuals who have contributed so vitally to this publication. Essentially a grassroots and voluntary project, this book has become a reality only through the sacrificial efforts of family and friends. Without their encouragement and suggestions, I might never have put my Christian testimony on paper. Thanks to all who have given me positive support for this writing.

Randy Mellinger has been indispensable in helping me with editing. His attention to detail and keen eyes have caught a myriad of my mistakes. Randy's support and encouragement have also lifted me emotionally and spiritually. His love for the Lord has been infectious as well. Thank you, Randy.

Doug Downer has turned a large computer draft into a format that looks like a book. His contacts in publishing and skills in computers have been essential. Many thanks, Doug, for giving time out of an already full schedule.

Without the financial contributions of friends and family, this book would not exist. The following people have contributed significant funds to the book's publication: Clay and Margie Miller, John and Debera Barco, Hartley and Lona Brown, Michael and Mary Lou Boydstun, Kurt and Peggy Freeman, and Jim Stitzinger III. The significant contribution of my grandmother, Mary Opal Keith, is greatly appreciated. My parents, Ed and Judy Watkins, are the chief underwriters of the book. Many thanks to all those above for making an investment that helped put my Christian testimony into print.

My family has had the greatest role in this project. My

parents-in-law, Dr. and Mrs. James Ramage, have given me valuable help and advice. They both assisted in proofreading the document, and their unceasing encouragement has given me essential momentum to keep writing. Dad and Mom have supported me in every way calculable. From their prayers to their financial support and more, they have manifested their love for me and confidence in me. Thanks, Dad and Mom. This is your book.

My wife, Andrea, has contributed to every page. Her proofreading and advice have been astute and accurate, and she has done this work while writing her own doctoral dissertation. Her love and support are a daily reminder of God's unfailing grace.

SOLI DEO GLORIA

INTRODUCTION

Trusting Jesus Christ for salvation as a United States Navy SEAL was the beginning of my greatest adventures. My testimony in the following pages tells how God saved me in an "unconventional" way and met me where I least expected Him—behind enemy lines. Ever since childhood the dream of my life was to become one of America's elite naval commandos, and the realization of my dream eventually turned into a personal quest for Jesus Christ. My story is a testimony to God's power in redeeming me. I would never have expected Him to deploy the combat zone as a backdrop for salvation, but God's ways continue to be a mystery.

Writing my testimony is in some ways a fearful task. To recall the events of my life without detracting from God's total control in every situation is challenging and perhaps, ultimately, impossible. The extraordinary events in my life and service as a Navy SEAL may sound as if I am due some credit for my achievements. That is in no way true. I readily acknowledge that anything I may have achieved in a positive way is directly a matter of God's grace working through my life and is not of my own merit. I have nothing about which to boast except that I, by God's grace, am able to know Him as my Savior and Redeemer. The parts of my testimony that may sound incredible or sensational are a result of a plan that God had made before I was born and had carried out in my life as He worked through me.

My goal in sharing the ways that God worked in my life and drew me to salvation is so that His name may be glorified. It is my desire that God would use my service as a SEAL as testimony of His marvelous grace. If one person seeks to give God honor because of my testimony, then it has been well worth the writing.

My story is really God's story. It is the recalling of how the bridge of God's grace was extended to me, even when I was dead in trespasses and sin. I hope and pray that readers will know that I could have done nothing without God's enabling power. I became a SEAL because God was pleased to choose that as my path for six intense years. He allowed me to pass the training, to become a SEAL, and even to write this book—all of which reflect His plan and grace in my life.

The testimony of my life and salvation is written as the events unfolded, and I made every effort to recount my feelings and convictions in chronological order. I had rejected the gospel of Jesus Christ early on in my life, in spite of a superficial profession of faith at a young age. Until I was saved, my mother was the only redeemed member of my immediate family. Although she had presented and encouraged the good news of Jesus, I rejected what light I had. But she persisted in praying for me for many years, and God answered her prayers in powerful and unexpected ways.

So as you read about exciting and somewhat remarkable experiences in my life, bear in mind that God is the One who planned them all; any accomplishments or successes that were achieved were not a result of my efforts or talents in any way. I do not know why God chose to do the fascinating things in my life that He did, but I do know that everything good was totally of Him, and everything bad was totally of me. Through my humble story I pray that your heart will be warmed and encouraged and that you will come to revere, as I have, the Lord Jesus Christ.

PART ONE
ENDURING AMBITION

1.

GROWING UP ON INDIANA JONES

Preparing for the mission was more fun than the mission itself. Donald Vish and I had received top secret orders and had been clearly briefed on actions at the objective area. We ritualistically climbed into our uniforms. For us, the uniform of the day was concealing camouflage that would effectively blend into Southeast Asian jungles. We were Green Berets on our way into the jungles of Vietnam to liberate a POW camp. At age ten, neither of us cared where Vietnam actually was, or that the war had been over for more than four years. We just knew that someone was waiting to be liberated, and we were the men for the mission. As boys, we saw ourselves as a couple of "good men" with esprit de corps, who were semper fidelis (the motto of the Marines, meaning "always faithful") and ready de opresso liber (the motto of the Army Green Berets, meaning "to free the oppressed").

As a typical red-blooded American lad, I had a typical red-blooded best friend, Donald Vish. Donald and I confided everything we knew to one another. We were official blood brothers in the Native American tradition; we were Jack London survivalists; and we conducted our crusades in the spirit of Indiana Jones. Our most common form of entertainment was military role-playing. However, we both harbored contempt for conventional forces such as, heaven forbid, the Army infantry. I don't know why we were so set on being different, but different we were. As "hopeless young romantics,"

Donald and I believed that to have a world of safety and peace there also had to be "special soldiers."

The usual dilemma we faced was in choosing which unconventional outfit we belonged to. For a long time, which at age ten could have been two weeks, we played out the roles of Marine Force Reconnaissance or Green Berets, and on occasion we became Army Rangers. But one day, Donald made a major discovery. Because his father had never allowed a television set in the house until Donald was in high school, entertainment at the Vish residence took the form of books. As Donald combed through war books, he ran across a picture of a United States soldier in Vietnam who broke all the military molds, even for Special Forces. The soldier's picture enchanted us. Squatting by a nipa palm and camouflaging himself with black pajamas like a Vietcong guerrilla, he wore an olive drab bandage around his head, Aunt Jemimah style, and clutched a weapon we had never seen before. His goatee quickly told us that he was not Marine Force Recon. His lack of the Special Forces tab, beret, and olive jungle greens told us that he wasn't a Green Beret either. We soon found out that the man was a U.S. Navy SEAL, the "most dreaded animal in the jungle," according to the caption. That did it! From then on, I hardly remember an occasion when Donald and I were anything but Navy SEALs.

Our fascination with SEALs grew as we grew, and my own preoccupation with these enigmatic warriors stimulated my imagination and possessed my thoughts. I began reading the sparse collection of books about SEALs at our school library. I asked nearly every older friend and cousin who had been in any way associated with the military if they would kindly tell me everything they knew about Navy SEALs, including their average shoe size. Most of the books in the school library that I got my hands on were about the Navy Underwater Demolition Teams (UDTs). Commonly called "Frogmen," UDTs are the ancestors of modern Sea, Air, and Land (SEAL) teams. Frogmen were the Navy's combat swimmers of World War II who had come ashore to prepare the beach lanes for amphibious landings. In the Second World War, UDT teams cleared the beaches of Normandy for the Allied invasions in France.

Desiring to follow the steps of the legendary UDT teams, Donald and I saved our money to buy an inflatable raft at the Western Auto store in La Grange, Kentucky. With a raft we would navigate the waters of Harrod's Creek, which eventually dumped into the Ohio River just a few miles upstream from Louisville. For Donald and me, girls had not yet replaced what were to us the two most fascinating natural elements: water and fire. Those were indispensable elements for SEALs as well. (Although a gun was to us the most tantalizing man made object, our parents wisely prohibited real guns from our possession.) Our fascination with water continued to grow because of our adventures with the raft, and our fascination with fire involved gasoline, gunpowder, and once, even Donald's attic. We often failed to see the "big picture" with fire and ended up learning some hard lessons in the fundamentals of thermal combustion. We are proof of God's divine intervention in human affairs for having spared both our lives on numerous occasions.

At some point, I became more committed than Donald about seriously trying out for the SEALs "in real life," as we would say. Nothing excited me like the thought of becoming a Navy SEAL. Football, baseball, academics, and everything else appeared lackluster to me, and I developed a sense that nothing in life would ever satisfy me like becoming a naval commando. I did not have the patience for Sir Walter Scott, but I strove to live a life matching the action in one of his novels.

Boyhood missions with Donald were some of the greatest, most idealistic times of my life. I treasure the memories of the numerous mock operations on which we embarked. They were truly adventurous times, and Harrod's Creek may as well have been the Amazon or Vietnam's Mekong. Every outing was full of excitement, and if no excitement presented itself, we would attempt to create a little with the resources of fire and water. But eventually we both outgrew the games and went our separate ways once we entered high school.

After high school, I enrolled in the University of Louisville for the fall semester of 1986, and after one semester, decided that school was not yet for me. Reading Louisville's Courier Journal one morning, I saw an article that read, "Navy's Divefarer Program Seeks SEALs." The article reported the Navy's program to double the number of SEALs by 1992 because of the Reagan administration's commitment to enlarge the commando outfits. I went promptly to the Navy recruiting offices and told them to take whatever means necessary to sign me up for "Divefarer." For the first time in my life, I was truly excited about the future. I felt free, young, unlimited, and bound for the goals that I had determined were important. Above all, I thought that, as a SEAL, I could make a difference in solving the problems of the world. My young, idealistic world was due to change rapidly.

2.

NAVY BOOT CAMP

Leaving the airport for Orlando, Florida, and Navy boot camp was a painful experience. The day I left for two months of recruit training, March 7, 1987, was a landmark change in my life. I do not usually show my emotions outwardly, but if I had looked back toward my family as I walked to the plane that day, tears would have been unavoidable. There they stood: Mom, Dad, my sister Sina, and Donald Vish. The thought that stirred my emotions the most was that they might think I was leaving for the Navy because I was tired of them. Nothing could have been farther from the truth, but the possibility of their thinking that broke my heart.

I was leaving because middle-class suburban America bored me to the point of oppressive grief. Commenting on the doldrums of middle-class suburban boredom, Philip Caputo wrote this in his memoir of Vietnam:

sleek, new schools smelling of fresh plaster and floor wax; supermarkets full of Wonder Bread and Bird's Eye frozen peas; rows of centrally heated split levels that lined dirtless streets on which nothing ever happened. It was pleasant enough at first, but by the time I entered my late teens I could not stand the place, the dullness of it, the summer barbecues eaten to the lulling drone of power mowers (A Rumor of War [New York: Ballantine Books, 1977], 4-5).

Those were my sentiments exactly! In that kind of environment, there was no way to continue the idealism and adventure that Donald and I had shared. The SEALs were my only hope of having "not just a job, but an adventure."

Navy boot camp was the most demoralizing experience of my life. I don't mean to take any potency away from the Army, Air Force, or Marines, but at least those services have uniforms that leave one with some measure of dignity. Navy uniforms, especially the working dungarees, may be strategically designed for practicality, but they also possess the inherent ability to make an otherwise attractive person look like a dork. We didn't even get to hold real guns at Navy boot camp, except at the pistol range, and even those were .22-caliber, not "real," guns.

Boot camp was less than physically challenging. I had already been running, swimming, and doing various calisthenics before boot camp to prepare myself for the SEAL physical screening test, which was to be administered at boot camp. The Navy workouts were less rigorous than the training I had already imposed on myself. My company commander (a Navy drill instructor) found out that I had volunteered for SEAL training. As he was punishing our company by making us crank out pushups, he noticed my uncontrollable smile. I loved it when he made us work out physically because that helped to prepare me further for the SEAL screening. He asked me why I was smiling, and when I told him the reason, he stated emphatically that SEALs were crazy. But he and I had a special relationship from then on. I think he respected me for the level of commitment that he knew I was giving to the Navy and to the country. He must have respected something about me because soon after that event I was made physical training (PT) petty officer of our boot-camp company, which meant that I led our company's calisthenics and runs. The other sailor recruits were not crazy about having me, a SEAL candidate, as the PT leader, but they did end up in good physical shape. The company commander also promoted me to section leader, firing the previous leader for incompetence. I remember feeling sorry for the person who had been fired. He was a nice guy and tried hard to be a good section leader, but he lacked the assertiveness needed to control a section of wild eighteen and nineteen year-old recruits.

What really carried me past the feelings of worthlessness at boot camp was seeing, for the first time, a fully qualified Navy SEAL. Our company went to the base swimming pool and Petty Officer Clem Lisor, the SEAL motivator on temporary assignment to the Recruit Training Center, gave us a sales pitch to gain SEAL volunteers. I hardly needed a sales pitch. When Lisor walked into the room, I thought my heart was going to stop. He was wearing khaki colored (UDT) swim trunks and a blue and gold SEAL T-shirt. His physique was something out of a triathlon magazine. As he spoke, his gleaming white teeth were sharply contrasted by his tan arms and face. He looked alert, powerful, and reserved, like the most controlled person I had ever seen. His look resembled the combination of a physician and a champion athlete. The appearance was that of grace under pressure. Words fail to describe exactly how Lisor appeared to me, but he was everything I thought a SEAL ought to resemble physically.

Seeing Lisor allowed me to understand that SEALs were human beings, and hearing his motivating speech about working in the sun, diving, and parachuting made me burst with excitement. Up to that time I had often thought that I was kidding myself in thinking I could become a Navy SEAL. But

I sensed that there was no turning back on my goal to become a SEAL, and frankly, the thought of wearing the ugly Navy dungarees and working on a "gray ghost" (ship) was enough to make me willing to sacrifice life itself in the pursuit of that goal.

Boot-camp graduation came, and even though the couple months of training seemed eter_nal, graduating made it all worthwhile. My parents and sister traveled all the way to Orlando to see me graduate and that meant the world to me. After graduation, we spent my only day of liberty at Disney World and went out for dinner. The next day, I was sent to Lakehurst, New Jersey, for "A" school training. There I learned a Navy technical specialty so that I would be prepared for ship duty in the likely event that I would quit SEAL training.

3.

THE CALM BEFORE THE STORM

Lakehurst, New Jersey, was only a temporary distraction on my way to Navy SEAL boot camp. For two months I was required to attend "PR" school to obtain an official Navy rating designator of aircrew survival equipmentman (PR, for parachute rigger, was the abbreviated designation). At first, I failed to understand why the Navy required me to learn about fighter aircraft, ejection seats, and life rafts to become an elite Naval commando. My reasoning questioned what any of those things had in common with SEAL training and commando tactics. Later, I was rudely reminded that only 25 to 35 percent of all qualified SEAL candidates graduate from Basic Underwater Demolition/SEAL Training (BUDS). The remaining majority of 65 to 75 percent of the men who wash out are sent to the regular Navy fleet to finish out their enlistments, or to start another line of naval specialization. But I refused to ever really enjoy PR school; I wanted to be a Navy SEAL.

The PR training seemed pointless because I was determined not to quit or wash out of BUDS. If I failed to make it through SEAL training, it would be from an injury that would also exempt me from further service to the Navy. Quitting SEAL training never entered my mind at Lakehurst, and I used my free hours during PR school as a great opportunity to equip myself for BUDS. The time I spent training after hours at Lakehurst played a major part in preparing me mentally and physically for what lay ahead.

Every day, after I had finished the required PR duties and had marched back to the barracks in formation for over one mile, the real training began. Stripping off my detestable dungarees, I put on my swim trunks, jungle boots, and T-shirt, and left the barracks for two hours of self-inflicted torture. At that time, I had little concept of the word pain and had no earthly idea just how far the human body could be pushed. After changing into boots and trunks, I set out for a grueling three-mile run through soft, sandy pine lots at the Naval Air Technical Training Center (NATTC). The July heat and humidity made the three miles seem endless. I attempted to simulate the circumstances of SEAL training by wearing boots and running in soft sand whenever possible.

The course for my runs was preplanned so that I would finish near the NATTC swimming pool, where phase two of my training occurred. A friend at PR school, who was himself a BUDS dropout, warned me far in advance of a brutal drill in BUDS called "drownproofing." He claimed that SEAL recruits must pass a test of swimming over two hundred yards, making descents and ascents in the deep end of the pool, while at other times, turning somersaults underwater. Included in the drill was a test in which the trainee must swim to the bottom of the deep end and pick up a face mask with his teeth only. The drill didn't sound too harsh until he added that it must all be done with the feet bound and hands tied together behind one's back. At first, the task sounded impossible, but I was soon to learn otherwise.

People looked at me strangely at the NATTC pool when I bound myself with ropes. I explained what I was about to do to the lifeguard at the pool and requested that, in the event I stayed underwater for over one minute, he please come in and get me. We probably broke some kind of rule at the pool; however, I saw no rules posted that prohibited swimming with one's own hands and feet tied. At least I wasn't guilty of breaking any posted rules. The lifeguard probably thought I was a little tilted in my judgment, but he accommodated me out of either sheer amusement or a deep-seated desire to make a rescue. With hands and feet bound, I began to swim, at first drinking lots of water from the pool. The swimming was absolutely hideous. I hated every minute of it. But eventually I became comfortable swimming tied up and achieved the endurance to swim about a mile that way.

Once the self-torture was over, I took a ten-minute break to dry off, don the jungle boots, and run one remaining mile back to the barracks. I usually made it in time to shower, change clothes, and catch a hot meal at the chow hall before it closed for the evening. The only drawback to arriving last for chow was that all the ripe bananas and good oranges had already been taken. I was usually left with an ugly apple or pear. Refusing to eat cake and ice cream, I have enjoyed fruit as a satisfying dessert ever since my days at Lakehurst.

In PR classes, which consisted of phases divided into parachutes, inflatable rafts, and sewing, I constantly daydreamed about SEAL training and missions. I would look at the parachutes we packed and think of being air-dropped into the Middle East on a secret mission. While glancing at an inflatable raft (one that was contained in a pilot's ejection seat), I imagined a rubber raiding craft full of commandos about to land upriver in Vietnam's Mekong Delta. I read every piece of SEAL literature I could find, learning about "Hell Week," the toughest part of SEAL boot camp. The books taught me about SEAL advanced training, closed-circuit scuba, arctic-warfare school, airborne school, and SEAL missions in Vietnam. At night, I would sit and stare at pictures of the Trident, the United States Navy SEAL insignia, consisting of an eagle holding a trident harpoon, and a gun with an anchor in the background. The insignia looked untouchable to me.

Days at Lakehurst were boring, evenings were rigorous, and nights were exceptionally restful. Spare time was spent wondering if I was cut out for SEAL training or if I was just kidding myself. On occasion, I would ride my motorcycle through Manhattan to just north of Bridgeport, Connecticut. There I spent free weekends with one of my best friends and high school buddies, Christian Edwards. We scraped together enough money to go deepsea fishing and talked endlessly about the melancholy feeling we both had after leaving our homes for the "real world." He kept my confidence high, telling me that he knew I could make it through the training yet to come. He will never know just how encouraging and timely his words were to me.

Lakehurst taught me many lessons, including those of patience and self-discipline. But perhaps the most valuable lesson was learning the importance of humility. It had dawned on me that the Navy was training me first as a sailor, because statistically, graduating from SEAL training was highly unlikely.

Although Lakehurst was a valuable time of mental and physical training, I look back on PR school as a semiromantic, idealistic phase of my life, which would soon be halted with the harsh reality of the most physically demanding training in the United States military. I met a few people at Lakehurst who said they had washed out of BUDS and even more people who had met an actual SEAL; however, except for Clem Lisor, whom I had met at boot camp, I didn't meet any more SEALs until I arrived at BUDS in San Diego.

After graduating from PR school, I packed my two "sea bags," loaded them onto my Honda Magna motorcycle, and took out across the "land of the free and home of the brave." Driving from just south of Manhattan to San Diego on a motorcycle was good SEAL training in itself. The ride was memorable and reflective, the calm before the storm.

PART TWO

RIGOROUS TRAINING

4

WELCOME TO BUDS

Basic Underwater Demolition/SEAL Training (BUDS) is the required twenty-six week course that is Navy SEAL boot camp. No amount of book learning, physical exercise, or psychological conditioning can prepare a man for BUDS. As of this writing, the United States Navy SEALs have never left a fallen SEAL behind enemy lines for the adversaries to capture, nor has there ever been any SEAL taken prisoner of war. BUDS is the chief cause behind such results. It is said that if a man won't quit in BUDS, he plain won't quit.

There is good reason BUDS is so rigorous, averaging a 70 percent attrition rate. The training is specifically designed by the Navy to produce a caliber of soldier who can be relied upon not to break in any situation, no matter how bad the cards are stacked against him. The training does not ensure that SEALs will be able to accomplish anything, but it pretty well ensures that SEALs will not give up in the process of trying to achieve a seemingly impossible feat. BUDS is the only way to produce this high caliber of soldier, and the great majority of those who try it fail.

As I arrived at BUDS on Coronado Island, California, in August 1987, a weird sense of ambiguity hit me. My motorcycle hummed slowly through streets with beautifully manicured lawns in spotless Coronado. After driving my bike for over two thousand miles and having time to reflect on a myriad of thoughts, my heart began to race as I knew I was less than one mile from BUDS and the headquarters of the West Coast SEAL teams. My emotions were mixed because, in the middle of this paradise of gorgeous seventy-degree weather and prestigious houses, there was a "hell" where I would be tested, pushed, broken, and tried in the face of the worst physical conditions imaginable. It just seemed surreal that the Coronado paradise was the home of the Navy's darkest nightmares. If two things in life ever seemed to conflict, it was the horror of BUDS and the beauty of Coronado.

Except for the frigid winter waters of the Pacific Ocean, Coronado had ideal weather for training. The mild, low-humidity climate failed, however, to counterbalance the rigors of SEAL training. If anything, the ideal climate allowed the body to be pushed to the maximum physical limits. My BUDS class started training in October 1987, and to this day I vividly remember the first conditioning run. Dressed in long, green Seabee pants, jungle boots, and white T-shirts, our class started to run in the soft white sands of the Coronado beach. I was a hundred paces into the run, and my lungs were already sucking for more air. Stings of pain began to shoot through my calves and thighs as I pushed myself to keep up with the instructor. The pace was incredibly fast, and all my physical and mental preparation at Lakehurst seemed to equal zero on that run. I remember reasoning that, if this was the first run at the slowest pace, there was no possible way that I could survive for six more months.

One of the staggering difficulties in BUDS training is that in every timed evolution (an evolution being any scheduled training exercise), one must improve his previous time. That means successive improvement in exercises such as running, swimming, and obstacle courses. The idea seemed insane. How could anyone continually improve his speed in all events? There had to be some limit, or so I thought. Our class had much to learn about the "power curve" and the "comfort zone." Staying ahead of the power curve meant always bettering one's previous time. The comfort zone meant running or swimming at a pace that didn't hurt in a physical and mental way, or in other words, any pace slower than one was capable of achieving. If we were staying in the comfort zone, we were not giving all that we had. We also had yet to learn the SEAL mottoes: "The only easy day was yesterday!"; "The pain that does not kill me makes me stronger!"; and my favorite, "The more you sweat in peace, the less you bleed in war."

And then there were the instructors. They were hardened SEALs who had experience and possessed physiques that resembled Greek statues. They were also intense. The job of the instructors was to separate the men from the boys and to present the SEAL teams with a crop of fresh commandos whom the instructors would be proud to accompany behind enemy lines. With that as the instructors' goal, it is easy to understand why they seemed so heartless and cruel at the time. In reality, it was not that they were heartless or cruel, but that they needed to weed out the BUDS candidates who might break mentally behind enemy lines and possibly endanger the whole squad.

The instructors pushed BUDS students to their physical and mental limits, which required the outpouring of some harsh displays of personality by the instructors. They would punish us with countless push-ups at the drop of a hat. After completing the push-ups, we were required to yell "Hoo-yah, Instructor." But we had to remain in the push-up position with our arms burning with pain until the instructor responded and allowed us to recover. Most of the time we were dropped for no reason, and the instructors would make us stay in the push-up position for a long time. They would also play mind games with us. One time I had completed some push-ups and yelled "Hoo-yah" while waiting for the word recover from the instructor. After hearing the word, I sprang to my feet. But immediately the instructor yelled for me to drop back down and asked me what I was doing. As I was explaining that I had heard the word recover, he interrupted me and said his words were reed cover. So I had to crank out another set of push-ups and wait several more minutes before I could stand up and rest my arms.

It might seem hard to believe, but humorous things occurred in the midst of training. Like so much of life, some of the funniest and most paradoxical moments took place in the heat of serious circumstances. Most of the humor, which incidentally was not all that funny for us as trainees at the time, was because of the instructors' incredible demands on the students. For example, after endless and grueling sessions of calisthenics in the sand, including push-ups, sit-ups, rope climbs, flutter kicks, and many other withering exercises, the instructors would say that everyone was not "putting out," meaning that we were not trying hard enough. Even though it sure felt like we were putting out, we were told as a class to make a sprint to the ocean, jump in, and get back to the place of our training (called the "grinder") in less than two minutes. After doing just that, we were told that we were too slow. The instructor then said, "You people move like a bunch of old women, and you had better start acting like you want to be here!" Perhaps the humor is not so obvious, but his statement was so blatantly untrue that, now looking back on it, I find it hysterical and wonder what real thoughts were going through our instructors' minds. There were times when the instructors had to turn away to keep from bursting into laughter and other times when the laughter was too spontaneous to control.

There was nothing funny about the training itself. BUDS is divided into three, two-month phases. First Phase is also called Physical Phase, during which students are pounded into shape with nearly round-the-clock physical training and harassment. Halfway through First Phase is Hell Week, the single most difficult week in BUDS. The goal of instructors in First Phase is to weed out as many people as possible before investing much time and money in students during the more expensive Second and Third Phases of training. Second Phase deals with training in land warfare, and Third Phase teaches students how to become combat swimmers and focuses on both open- and closed-circuit scuba. (Currently, the order of training in Second and Third Phases is reversed from when I was in BUDS training; that is, training in combat swimming and diving is now Second Phase, and training in land warfare is now Third Phase.)

The initial half of First Phase was a warm-up for Hell Week and was the most rigorous physically and mentally. Harassment by instructors was intense, as were long conditioning runs in the soft sand, two-mile swims in the open ocean, grueling obstacle courses, extended drills with rubber rafts, endless calisthenics, and more. Those daily activities caused many people to quit SEAL training in the weeks leading up to Hell Week. To quit, one was required to ring a brightly polished bell three times at the BUDS compound, announcing his status as a quitter. Often the class was made to sing "Happy Trails" to the individual who had quit. The whole process of BUDS was more or less one of constant humiliation.

The depths of my own humiliation in the weeks leading up to Hell Week occurred on a conditioning run. This run took place during the first full week of Phase One. The instructors started out the run at a fast pace, and the pace only continued to increase for the duration. I was an average runner at the beginning of BUDS training, but this particular run was so fast that only two or three persons in the whole class were able to keep up with the instructor. The rest of the class dropped back, spreading out to cover about a one-mile stretch of beach. The instructors would target groups that dropped back on the run to engage them in some extra harassment called the "goon squad." People in the goon squad were made to do all kinds of hideous extra feats like getting totally wet in the ocean and then rolling in the soft sand to become a "sugar cookie." Then push-ups, sit-ups, eight-count body builders, and other torturous calisthenics followed.

I happened to be caught in a "goon squad" on that one insidious run, along with all but about five guys. But instead of getting wet in the ocean, I was forced to run and jump into a stagnant pit of trapped tidewater. The water stank, and I remember seeing a dead fish floating in the still water. After being completely covered with putrid water, I had to crawl out and cover myself with sand. Next, the instructor made me do push-ups until my arms were burning and had reached muscle failure. When I could push no further, the instructor ordered me to grab a mouthful of sand and hold it in my mouth while I attempted to run and catch the rest of the class. Of course, that was nearly impossible, and globs of sand and saliva ran down the sides of my mouth as I pushed on to catch the class. All the while the instructor yelled, "Open your mouth; I want to see that sand!" If I drooled some of the sand out of my mouth, I had to drop down and scoop in more sand to satisfy the instructor, who continued to demand that I show him the mouth full of sand as I ran to catch the class.

Eventually I made it to the rest of the class, and the instructor began harassing someone else. At that point, I made a vow with myself that I would never again fall back on a run, and that was the last time I was ever "goon squaded." Later in SEAL training I became one of the top five runners in my class, and I have always thought that my primary motivation in becoming a fast runner was that unpleasant mouthful of sand.

BUDS shattered the dreams and glamour of being a SEAL with harsh reality. The serious demands of what commandos had to endure smacked me right in the face every dark morning at 4:30, when the alarm clock jolted me out of a warm rack. A typical First Phase day began by hurriedly preparing for a four-mile timed run in the sand. After the "gut-busting" run, a mile run to breakfast and another one-mile run back to the BUDS compound would ring in the light of day. The next event was PT on the grinder. This midmorning agenda consisted of push-ups, pull-ups, sit-ups, dips, flutter kicks, eight-count body builders, ad infinitum. Running one mile to and from lunch prepared us for the two-mile timed ocean swim. Students run six miles per day just going to and from meals. Next on the day's lively schedule was "Log PT," which involved boat crews (usually seven men) collectively doing a variety of exercises with telephone poles. For example, lying on our backs with the poles on our stomachs, we would do sit-ups. From a standing position, we lifted the poles head high and then lowered them from one shoulder to the other. After Log PT, it was time to run a mile to and from dinner. After dinner, we had team races to see which crew could paddle inflatable rafts (called IBSs) the fastest. The physical results of the paddling included cramped back muscles and sore triceps. As I later learned, those boat races were a warm-up for Hell Week. The close of the evening was spent cleaning uniforms, squaring away the barracks, and finally trying to get some sleep for reveille at 4:30 A.M. and another "easy day." To think that there were twenty-six weeks of these days was nearly unbearable.

BUDS training produces in students who complete the program is an amazing tenacity and "fire in the gut" that will refuse to quit and that will face any obstacle, no matter how difficult. As First Phase continued toward the climax of Hell Week, every day got harder, the runs faster, and the water colder. The unwelcome specter of November finally came and so did the dark cloud of Hell Week. This week, like no other week in my life, took me face-to-face with every facet of my human will.

5.

HELL WEEK

What was an otherwise pleasant November Sunday afternoon began the longest and most intense week of SEAL training and of my life. Hell Week began on the fifth week of BUDS and was designed to force the trainees who hadn't yet quit to reconsider the cost of becoming a Navy SEAL. The tactic worked! Nearly forty persons quit during our Hell Week, and this chapter is testimony to some of the reasons they did so, and why all SEAL candidates have considered quitting at least once during this week-long nightmare.

Sunday was uneventful, but the stressful anticipation of the coming night's activities was overwhelming. "Breakout," which is like the opening ceremony of Hell Week, was set to occur about 9:00 P.M. Our class was instructed to dress in the regular training attire of green long-sleeved shirts, long pants, jungle boots, and baseball style caps. We were also ordered to stay in the barracks until further notification. The nervousness during those evening hours of waiting were intense and seemed endless.

After about three long hours of waiting, we were "notified" by the ear-splitting thumps of grenade simulators, M-60 machine guns, and the yelling commands of enraged instructors blasting from bull horns. At first, the scenario seemed unreal and nearly animated, but it did not take long for the gravity and reality of the situation to set in. We ran back and forth to the rapid commands from instructors, completing

[handwritten annotation: LYING ON BACK / KICKING LEGS]

countless push-ups, sit-ups, flutter kicks, and other tiring exercises. I felt invincible initially, for we were in great physical shape from a solid month of grueling Phase One workouts. During the first two hours of harassment my heightened adrenaline levels made me feel like a machine that could not be exhausted. But that feeling went away after another long hour of pounding calisthenics.

THE TEST OF SURF TORTURE

At midnight, I began to feel tired, and my dreams of invincibility came crashing down when our class was ordered into the frigid waters of the Pacific Ocean for "surf torture." This painful evolution involved walking knee-deep into the ocean, then turning to face the beach in one long line. As our class was strung out parallel to the beach, we interlocked our elbows and sat down in the water in synch with the instructor's command. As we sat down, the water came up to our necks. Wave after wave washed over our heads and shoulders and chilled us to the bone. The rushing waters sucked the heat out of our tired bodies. The painful cold seemed unbearable as we shivered uncontrollably and began to lose body heat and dexterity. At the point when our speech became slurred, the beginning stages of hypothermia, instructors would bring us back onto the beach and engage us in more push-ups, sit-ups, and flutter kicks to restore our bodies to normal temperature. Surf torture was just plain misery as our shirts and pants clung to our skin, and sand worked its way into every place where skin rubbed on skin.

Probably no single event in Hell Week or in BUDS caused more people to quit than surf torture. The cold water had a way of absolutely breaking the will to fight. Time seemed to stand still as we sat in the cold waters attempting not to move. Movement seemed to cause pain as water shifted into the few remaining warm parts of our bodies, like the armpits and chin. Those areas of the body had a way of intensifying the effects of the cold when water contacted them. I remember staring into the night sky watching naval planes make slow rolling approaches to Naval Air Station North Island on Coronado. I imagined what it would be like to be a pilot, warm and dry in his aircraft. I can't fully express the psychological and physical misery of surf torture, which is typically the most vivid scar in the mind of anyone who has suffered through Hell Week. Surf torture and calisthenics continued into the early hours of Monday morning.

At approximately 3:00 A.M., we were ordered to run across the strand separating BUDS from the Naval Amphibious Base. Nearly everywhere we went, we carried inflatable boats (IBSs) on our heads. Those rafts weighed about 250 pounds apiece, and they thrashed our neck muscles as we ran. After running over one mile with the pounding boats, we came to a halt at a steel pier that jutted into the San Diego Bay. Our class stood in ranks on the steel pier, and the order was given for us to strip off all our clothes, except the spandex triathlon shorts that we wore as underwear. The air temperature was in the low fifties, and the ocean water was sixty degrees. Just standing without clothes chilled us as the wind made contact with our bare skin. We were then told to lay down with our backs flat on the cold steel pier. It felt so cold at first that I thought my skin was going to stick to the metal. The unbearable cold was intensified when instructors began spraying a cold mist of water over our shaking bodies with a hose. I could hear the knock of bones hitting steel as we shivered uncontrollably.

To warm up, we were ordered to jump into the bay. At a normal body temperature, that would have felt like a freezing plunge. But after the treatment on the pier, the bay water felt refreshingly warm. As soon as our skin temperatures adjusted to the sixty-degree water, however, we slowly began to feel cold again. Even though the water was warmer than the cold mist and wind on the steel pier, the water was still well below a temperature suitable to the human body. About the time we began to feel cold again, the instructors pulled us out of the water for more torture on the pier. Again the cold spray felt intense, and again uncontrollable shaking resulted. I had never imagined that shivering could be so painful, and our muscles started to cramp from involuntary response to the intense cold. The extreme chill from surf torture became physically exhausting, as well as painful and demoralizing. I remember the instructors saying that we could secure the evolution if one person quit. Someone did quit, but the evolution continued on.

THE TEST OF WHISTLE DRILLS

Eventually, we were ordered to put our WET clothes back on and assemble in ranks, with the heavy boats on our heads. Throughout Hell Week we worked in seven-man boat crews. At first the rafts seemed bearable, but after we had been running, lifting, and doing other strenuous training for hours, the rafts seemed to weigh a ton. What's more, the instructors would occasionally fill our rafts with sand and water to make them twice as heavy. At other times we were required to hold the raft over our heads, with arms extended, for lengthy periods of time. That exercise caused our arm muscles to cramp severely and, ultimately, to reach a point of collapse. It took all seven men straining to bear the load of an IBS, and if one person in a boat crew quit, the team had one less man to carry the load. So the load became exponentially heavier as men dropped out and Hell Week continued. We moved out, carrying the rafts, and the pounding in our necks and backs resumed. For over one mile, we ran the boats back to the BUDS compound, where we spent the rest of the darkness doing "whistle drills."

Whistle drills became a dreaded occurrence. When an instructor blew his whistle once, we had to respond by "hitting the deck" belly-down. Two blasts and we had to "low crawl" on our arms and legs toward the whistle, scraping our stomachs on the ground. In the sand, this was a torturous activity. It not only was strenuous, cumbersome, and exhausting, but also filled every crack and crevice of clothing with small amounts of abrasive sand. Around the waist and belt, under armpits, inside the collar, and in boots, the sand caused intense chaffing, bleeding, and plenty of pain. The sores were continually irritated throughout the week, and the soreness was intensified from constantly sprinting in and out of the salty ocean water. As the water entered the raw chaffed areas, the salty burn compounded our discomfort.

As the whistle blew, we crawled frantically toward the sound of the beeps-up hills, over sand berms, and even across pavement. This was an exhausting drill, especially since we had been through constant harassment since 9:00 the previous evening. It was now about 5:30 on Monday morning, and the sun began to emerge as both an enemy and a friend. In a friendly way, the sun warmed us a little, adding the positive feelings that usually accompany sunshine. But as an enemy, it reminded us of the immutable timetable to which we were all forced to submit. It was only Monday morning! I felt like I had no strength left inside me, and we had to keep going until Friday evening, with no breaks and no sleep. At that point, I began to wonder what on earth I had gotten myself into and thought that I had taken on more than I could handle. As the hours passed slowly, the intensity of the harassment and the physical demands placed upon us seemed to increase rather than decrease. Our increased physical fatigue from constant drilling and lack of sleep only made matters seem more grim. There was no light, and we could not even see the end of the tunnel.

THE TEST FOR BOAT CREWS

The week contained countless drills and competitions between boat crews. Nearly everything we did was a race to see which crew was the fastest. Boat crews that lost races or finished toward the back of the class were forced to do more calisthenics and were often punished with surf torture. The repetitive saying of the instructors was, "It pays to be a winner, gentlemen." The phrase meant that if one's boat crew didn't win a race, punishment was the result. The most common boat races were in the open ocean, where we could paddle furiously against other crews for miles. The instructors would follow us in four-wheel-drive trucks along the beach, marking the finish line by blinking the truck's headlights at us. At times during the paddling it seemed like we were standing still, but our cramped arm muscles told us differently. The intense burning in my triceps and back pounded away as we dug our paddles into the water in an effort to be "winners."

On Monday morning, after breakfast, we had a long boat race. Starting at Coronado Island, the race took us seven miles south to Imperial Beach. The race seemed never-ending as the miles drug on. Our boat crew was safely in the middle of the pack, as a string of IBSs could be seen for about a half mile. When we reached Imperial Beach, the instructors signaled to us, using the truck headlights, to paddle ashore. Because of a steep beach gradient and large November sea swells, the waves ranged in size from six- to eight-feet high, and they plunged with thundering crashes in the surf zone (the area where waves break). The power and size of the waves caused all the rafts to capsize. Eventually the whole class made it onto the beach and stood facing the instructors in ranks.

I recall counting about ten persons who quit during the next evolution. The drill was called "surf passage," and the objective was simple enough, in theory. Our boat crews had to paddle the IBS rafts from the beach to beyond the surf zone. The frequency and size of the waves caused the task to be nearly impossible. As we paddled with great intensity, one wave could launch our 250-pound raft and all seven boatcrew members into the air. Paddles would crack us in the forehead, and sometimes the waves would hold us underwater for up to a minute. After being smashed and scattered by the fierce waves, we would swim our way to the beach to regroup and make another of countless futile attempts to break through the mighty waves. Only one boat crew made it past the surf zone. And on that one occasion, it was because of an abnormally low set of waves from three- to five-feet high. Even then, the crew barely escaped being capsized.

The quitting began in earnest during surf passage. Students actually formed a line to quit for fear of the waves. To quit, individuals had to ring a bell three times in front of the class and walk shamefully to the instructors for a ride back to the base. The waves were so powerful and intimidating that they seemed to begin breaking some people's will to fight. One after another, students came up to quit rather than paddle against the breakers. Surf passage lasted all afternoon, and afterward, we went for a two-mile run, with boats on top of our heads, along the beach back toward Coronado Island. The instructors stopped us along a lonely stretch of the Silver Strand beach where we spent the night being harassed. The sun set on Monday night as we were again "surf tortured."

The Toll of Hell Week

Most sunsets bring beauty and warm thoughts. The first sunset in Hell Week, however, had a defeating effect on many of the trainees. Student after student began to quit. As the sun disappeared on the horizon, so did our motivation when we began a second long night of darkness and harassment, with four more endless days to go. Any positive thoughts that we once had were snatched away by the encompassing darkness. Yet another line of people formed to ring the bell. For a time, there didn't seem to be anything standing in the way of the whole class quitting. Somehow the psychological effects of seeing the sun vanish ushered despair and defeat into our hearts. Pondering four more days of that same misery and knowing that we were not yet twenty-four hours into Hell Week nearly broke my will to continue.

Through it all, something inside me—some "fire in the gut"—prompted me to keep pushing on until morning. Another grueling endless night of low crawling, surf torture, and calisthenics brought me to Tuesday morning. By Tuesday evening my mind was not altogether coherent. For example, I had an increasingly difficult time concentrating on details, and my thoughts wandered easily. My eyes became swollen and red, and stung every time I blinked. The drastic sleep deprivation began to wear away at one's will and ability to resist.

The lack of sleep also began to take a more serious toll, causing most of us to hallucinate and forget entire segments of time. I can recall almost nothing about Wednesday, Thursday, and Friday of that week, except what is brought back disjointedly through other classmates or written accounts. A few fragmented occurrences come to mind, but I do not trust my memory enough to put those recollections into words because they are foggy and unsequential. If the reader would like to know more about Hell Week, I suggest reading Douglas C. Waller's excellent book The Commandos: The Inside Story of America's Secret Soldiers (New York: Simon & Schuster, 1994). That book is not only about SEALs, but also about other current special-operations units. It is one of the finest and most objective critiques of modern United States military special operations in print. Waller, a correspondent for Newsweek, was allowed to observe a BUDS Hell Week, and his book contains an accurate chapter on the inside story of that subject.

The week dragged on and became an almost psychedelic sort of nightmare. By the end of the week I was so battered and hurt that my body required months to heal and recover fully from the resulting stress and damage. My feet were swollen from water retention and felt like they were about to split the leather of my jungle boots. Chaffing from sand had rubbed my armpits, groin, and waistline raw. Sores and some minor scarring occurred from the intense rubbing. One residual effect of Hell Week was the inability to feel warm. There were times after that week when I was completely covered with wool blankets and still on the verge of shivering.

Finally, Friday came, and our class, now a shadow of its original size, was officially secured from Hell Week. With close to forty quitters in the past week, I was amazed that I was still among the class. There were only about twenty-five to thirty persons remaining at the conclusion.

Hell Week came and went, although that week seemed like one year. Why some of us made it through the week without giving up is still somewhat of a mystery to me. But I believe a key reason I made it through was because I never looked too far ahead and was able to keep my own imagination and emotions in check. I respected the instructors, but I did not cower from, or fear, them. If I feared anything, it was failure itself. Nothing scared me more than the thought of looking in the mirror and seeing a quitter for the rest of my life. I have yet to face anything in life equal to the intensity of Hell Week. On many future SEAL operations, the internal tenacity gained during that week kept SEALs from giving up on some extremely tough missions. Although nearly five months of BUDS training remained, the worst single week was behind me.

6.

LAND WARFARE PHASE

After First Phase, BUDS became more interesting as it focused on SEAL small-unit tactics and weapons training. Once the instructors were convinced that we weren't going to quit, they began to teach us how to be SEALs. Second Phase consisted of land warfare tactics. Training involved maneuvers that are the bulk of what SEALs do on actual missions. Instruction included map and compass navigation, weapons and explosives proficiency, ambush tactics, underwater demolition tactics, rappelling, and mission planning. All the skills learned in Second Phase are combined for the Final Training Exercise (FTX) toward the end of the phase. The second half of the phase is spent on San Clemente Island, just west of Santa Catalina Island, off the Southern California coast. San Clemente provided live-weapons and demolition ranges and plenty of beach on which to practice maritime commando tactics.

Although no single week was as tough as Hell Week, parts of Second Phase seemed nearly as bad. The physical demands were even more rigorous than First Phase since required times for runs, swims, and obstacle courses got progressively faster. After physical training, we had to keep our minds calm and collected to safely manipulate explosives and weapons. Intense classroom lectures on explosive-charge computations and detonating systems required mathematical calculations and constant attentiveness. We also memorized

many intricate parts on various weapons, including nomen-
clature and statistics, and conducted disassembly and assem-
bly drills. The drills required completely taking apart different firearms and then reassembling them in a short span of
allotted time.

In many ways, Second Phase was my hardest phase. Even
though the intensity of Hell Week is unparalleled, it is only
one week. A common saying among BUDS students is, "I
could do one-arm push-ups for one week"; in other words,
compared to six months of harassment, one week is relatively short. Some of my greatest trials during BUDS took place
in Second Phase. Even after Hell Week, two persons quit during this phase, and a number of individuals were disenrolled
for performance deficiencies and safety violations.

BRAVING THE COLD AT CAMP ELIOT

During Land Warfare Phase, I began sensing the need for
God's comfort for the first time in my life. Using circumstances beyond my control, God began to open my eyes to
spiritual matters. Initially, though, I had no clear idea of what
I needed, but faced an overwhelming realization of my own
mortality and sensed a lack of power in the face of potentially fatal training exercises.

One of the harshest trials in SEAL training followed after
a day of rappelling and land navigation. One day our BUDS
class spent the morning and early afternoon learning to rappel
from the cliffs of Mission Gorge, California. When we finished the rapelling practice, our class was divided into seven-
man boat crews, and we were instructed to find a designated
location on our maps that was several miles away. It took us
the remainder of the afternoon to reach the location, and once

there, we set up Camp Eliot. We were scheduled to spend three days and two nights at this camp, conducting land warfare exercises such as fire-and-movement drills, booby trap courses, and basic patrolling tactics. But this short amount of time, which ended up being less than two days, turned into a mini-Hell Week. What made Camp Eliot seem like Hell Week was the cold. After our boat crews patrolled to a lay-up site, we spent the night in a concealed position. About half of the squad secured a 360-degree perimeter around our site. That is the same tactic used on a real mission. While three persons stayed awake on guard duty, four persons slept.

Two problems caused my night in the lay-up to be inconceivably miserable. The first was a record-breaking cold front that brought temperatures below freezing, which was rare for this part of Southern California. The second was my lack of a sleeping bag. I hasten to add, however, that I was willing and inclined to bring a sleeping bag along with me, as other members of my squad had done. But after much intersquad deliberation, a "command decision" was ultimately made by our squad leader. It was decided that if we minimized the amount of gear, and thus reduced our total weight, we could travel more rapidly and efficiently as a squad.

Since I was a radioman, which meant that I carried the weighty PRC-77 radio, it was determined that I didn't need to bring my sleeping bag. Once it was my turn to sleep in the lay-up, someone who was on guard would lend me their bag. So the M-60 gunner, the pointman, and I all left our sleeping bags back at the BUDS compound. Had I known beforehand of the misery that was about to ensue, I would have gladly carried the extra sleeping bag.

As our boat crew set security in the lay-up, I knew it was going to be an excruciatingly cold night. The three of us without sleeping bags got the first watch, which lasted from 11:00 P.M. to 2:30 A.M. To say that those of us on first watch nearly died of exposure is probably understating the case. I don't even remember surf torture being as bad as that one night in the lay-up site. For a time, I thought the pessimistic side of my mind was making it out to be worse than it really was. But that notion slowly eroded as I shivered uncontrollably while watching the accumulation of frost on surrounding bushes. I had an extra pair of socks in my rucksack, and I put them on my hands as makeshift mittens. Other than the socks on my hands, I was wearing pants, a shirt and field jacket, boots, and a baseball-style cap. I did not despair, however. The seconds were counting down to the time when my watch would be over and I could use a sleeping bag.

Eventually my watch was over, but I never got the luxury of a sleeping bag. The guys who were assuming the next watch, who had sleeping bags, refused to give up theirs because of the intense cold. Teamwork was always stressed in SEAL training, but the human instinct of self-preservation often overrules the forced instinct of teamwork. I like to think that if I had been the one in possession of a sleeping bag, I would have given it to the other person. But I honestly don't know if I would have because none of the other squad members gave up their bags that night. So the three of us without bags spent the night huddled together like a bunch of sled dogs, shaking uncontrollably the entire morning and not getting a wink of sleep. It was literally too cold to sleep. When the sun came up, I was so stiff that I didn't know if I could stand upright. I was unable to feel my feet and thought I had some minor frostbite, but that turned out not to be the case.

The following day at Camp Eliot, I could not stand with a straight posture. My lower back was cramped severely from carrying the heavy radio, as well as from the effects of the intense cold. All the drills and exercises were done with my upper body hunched over. I made an effort not to attract any attention from the instructors for fear that they would send me to medical and that I would possibly be "rolled back" and not be allowed to continue with my BUDS class. There was a slim chance of that happening, but I didn't want to take the risk. The next evening at Eliot, the instructors made the decision to leave the camp and return to the BUDS compound, cutting the training short by one whole day and night. The decision was made because afternoon rains threatened to raise lowlying creeks to levels that were impassable for vehicles. Those rains were a godsend because I honestly don't know if I could have survived another night of freezing temperatures.

During Land Warfare Phase, I had the privilege of being trained by one of the most knowledgeable and heroic Vietnam-era SEALs still on active duty. His name is Mike Bailey, now a retired master chief petty officer. Only his character and compassion as a friend exceed his abilities and talents as a SEAL. Mike was a hero to all the students, who constantly exchanged stories and rumors with one another about his many missions in Vietnam. Having served as a point man in Vietnam, Mike earned widespread respect in the SEAL teams. He has received numerous medals for combat heroism, including the Bronze Star and Purple Heart. Also notable were his missions working with his German shepherd, Prince, in Vietnam. But students also respected Mike because he didn't needlessly hammer them by requiring uncalled-for calisthenics as punishment. Instead, he treated us as future commandos and incorporated his real-combat analogies in some of the lessons. I always believed that I was in the presence of greatness when I was around Mike, and still do. But little did

I know, at that time, that I would eventually be in a SEAL platoon with him, and we would become lifelong friends. Mike was one of the prime reasons I endured SEAL training. When times were too tough, I reminded myself that someday I could be like Instructor Bailey. He even took me aside during Second Phase to encourage me to keep going at a time when I was having painful flare-ups with my knee. Fortunately, Mike was assigned to the group of instructors involved with my class.

TRAINING ON SAN CLEMENTE ISLAND

Second Phase pressed on, and it seemed as if every tough obstacle or encounter was supplanted by another that was even more arduous. At the same time, our class was becoming rock-hard physically and iron-willed mentally. I began to believe that we were indestructible and that no obstacles or limitations could keep us from achieving whatever task was placed before us. However, what came at San Clemente Island, during the last half of Second Phase, not only would be an obstacle to passing BUDS, but also would cause me to look beyond myself for help and strength. Through a course of events, God began moving in my life to humble me and start drawing me to Himself in salvation.

San Clemente Island is a lovely and serene place. The island has its own sort of desolate beauty which, if it were a song, would be set in a minor key. The green rolling hills are reminiscent of Ireland. Steep cliffs tower hundreds of feet above the rippling surface of the Pacific Ocean and are spectacular and awesome to behold, especially at night. To stand on the eastern side of the island at the top of the cliffs and look out at the peaceful nighttime ocean is breathtaking.

Since the waves are smaller on the eastern side and the cliffs are high above the water, the location is also quiet. The full moon causes the whole ocean to light up, creating a scene that only the poet Wordsworth could adequately describe.

San Clemente Island is beautiful, but like Coronado, it is also the location of some dour training. For example, before every meal we were required to complete one of two sets of draining physical tasks, alternating the tasks between meals. After successfully completing either chore, one had usually lost the desire to eat. The first prerequisite to a meal was called the "frog run." At the top of a steep hill, which was about a quarter mile in length, stood a huge statue of a frog, commemorating the "Frogmen" of World War II fame. A designated time was given for the students to sprint to the top of the hill and touch the frog statue. I don't recall the number of seconds we had to complete the run, but I do remember that if we did not sprint for all our worth, failure to make the cut-off time resulted. If we failed to make the time, we were required to "hit the surf," getting completely soaked, and then to eat a cold MRE ration (Meals Ready-to-Eat) while sitting outside the chow hall.

The other premeal activity involved climbing up and down a high rope, executing up to twenty good pull-ups, and finishing with twenty good dips. (Dips are an exercise where one lowers and raises his entire body weight with the arms while suspended on parallel bars.) Failure to complete any of those exercises resulted in the surf-zone and MRE treatment. Before every meal—breakfast, lunch, and dinner—we had either the frog run or the drill involving ropes, pull-ups, and dips. Alternating those tasks three times a day, every day, for one month—in addition to all the normal physical activity—added to our fatigue. Not even eating a meal was easy in

SEAL training. I guess the instructors were trying to make up for our not having to run two miles for every meal as we had done back in Coronado.

The most difficult test at San Clemente was "obstacle loading." Everyone in the class struggled with that event more than anything else at the island. Obstacle loading involved placing explosive charges underwater on man-made antiship obstacles. The obstacles were concrete "Japanese scullies" with iron bars sticking out of the concrete. They were usually located at rather shallow depths, depending on the tides. The test involved holding one's breath, swimming down with a satchel charge full of explosives, and securing the charge to the obstacle. At a twenty- to thirty-foot depth, the test was no easy feat. In addition, our wetsuits caused us to become as buoyant as corks, making it difficult just to swim down to the obstacle, much less to tie the appropriate knots in the correct sequence. The chain of adjustments that were required to attach the explosives successfully was a vital part of the test, and instructors graded us on every move. We worked in two-man pairs and were graded with a pass or fail evaluation. Failure to complete the task would result in having to take the obstacle-loading practical again. If a student failed the second time, he would likely be disenrolled. The pressure was high to perform the dreaded task.

Two additional factors made the drill difficult. On the day that our class was tested, the scullies had not been delivered to San Clemente. Therefore, we had to simulate the exercise by attaching the explosives to the pillars of a pier instead of the actual obstacles. Since there was a lack of ocean surge in the pier area, the instructors decided to increase the difficulty factor by placing the obstacles about ten feet deeper than usual. As we grabbed hold of the barnacle-covered pier, the sharp crustaceans sliced into our hands, causing sharp pain when the salt water contacted the open cuts. The difficult task caused butterflies to form in my stomach as we lined up on the pier to begin the painful process.

Waiting to be called down for the practical, our class was in formation and grouped in pairs on the topside of the pier. My partner and I were located toward the end of the line of students, and we had a long nervous period of waiting before being called onto the lower deck where pairs were evaluated. From our location, we could see down on the lower level where the instructors were standing, and some classmates were already beginning the test. Suddenly, I heard the instructors yelling, "Corps-man! Get a corpsman over here!" Everyone's heart rate rose instantly. I looked down at the lower deck and saw one of the first students lying on his back, completely blue and unconscious. He looked dead. The corpsman tried to revive him, and the student eventually began coughing up water. He turned out to be OK, but shaken up. The rest of us stood paralyzed by all the excitement. I felt like I had no energy and wondered how I would ever get through this test. As classmates continued the test, I slowly regained my outward composure. About five minutes later, the shout came again. "Corpsman!" I didn't even want to look, but my eyes were pulled to the excitement. There on the pier was another classmate out cold. He, too, looked pale and lifeless. After some treatment, he was coughing water and shaken like the previous student. My heart was racing again. I felt like saying, "Forget it! SEAL training is not worth my life or my sanity." But I also knew that I would never give up.

For the first time in BUDS, I truly believed my life was in danger. On that pier I cried out to God, to a God I did not yet know, asking Him for help to get me through the test. My prayer was simple, but desperate. In my mind I prayed, "Please help me, God. Give me strength." A sense of calm came over me as if everything was going to be fine. From that point on, I began thinking about God, wondering if He heard me and would respond to my prayers. It was when I believed that my life was in danger that I realized the world could offer me no comfort. My only option was to call out to God. As time went on and I experienced similar low points in my life, I somehow knew there was a God. I didn't know much about His character and Person then, but I did know that He existed. Just knowing that gave me a reason to find comfort. But it would take His moving in my heart before I was willing to submit to Him as Savior.

My turn finally came to load the obstacle. After waiting for what seemed like an endless time, I felt numb and expected the worst. I swam the obstacle down for the first series of tasks, and everything seemed to go wrong. The knots wouldn't tighten down, and my "swim buddy" (my assigned swimming partner), who was later kicked out of BUDS, failed to complete some of his tasks because he was running out of air. That left his unfinished work for me to complete, in addition to a whole new series of maneuvers. At the time, the cuts from the razor-sharp barnacles felt like little bee stings. But a day later, my hands were so sore from infections in the tiny slices that it was grueling to clench my fists. When I did, they cracked and bled, adding a new source of pain to the premeal rope climbs and pull-ups. My partner and I finished loading our obstacle and received a passing grade. We also managed to stay conscious throughout the ordeal.

Traversing Treacherous Waters

As Second Phase progressed, we grew physically and mentally hard. The ocean became less intimidating to us because of swimming countless miles in the chilly waters. The longest swim in BUDS was 5.5 nautical miles, which is equivalent to 6.3 standard miles. In preparation for the five-miler, we regularly swam a three-and-a-half-mile swim, as well as the routine two-mile timed swims. During one warm-up swim of three and one-half miles, storms arose, causing inclement conditions. Instructors on safety boats could not even see the swim pairs unless the boats were right alongside the students. As I swam, the wind whipped salt water into my mouth, which made it difficult for me to breathe. Finally, our class was recalled halfway through the swim and instructed to return to the launch point. But by returning to our original starting place, we ended up swimming the full distance after all.

The five-mile swim was an experience that seemed surreal. We arose at 3:00 A.M. to prepare for the marathon event. Getting out of bed was always brutal because of our constant exhaustion. As I slipped my bare feet onto the barrack's cold concrete floor, I knew that it was going to be a long day. After eating as much food as we could, we put on our swim gear and filed into ranks in the pitch-dark San Clemente fog. We were herded aboard a flatbed truck and were driven to our starting point, a pier several miles south of the BUDS camp. The instructions were easy enough: swim north, hugging the coast, until we reached the BUDS camp. We walked out on the dark lonely pier, and with our swim buddies, made a long plunge into the cold waters of the Pacific. The water for our swim was fifty-six degrees, and the initial submersion gave me an instant "ice-cream" headache.

The swim started out slow. The rising sun gave me hope that the nightmarish swim would eventually end. As usual, sunlight warmed my spirits. We swam, and swam, and continued to swim. Every time we rounded a section of coastal cliffs, I expected to see the BUDS camp. Dolphins and seals periodically swam with us, playing and jumping only an arm-length away. The animals were frustrating to watch as they swam at incredible speeds with little effort. Hours later, the long swim came to an end, and we made it to the BUDS compound. When we crawled out of the ocean onto the beach, it took several minutes before we could stand upright because of the stiffness in our legs. One of the instructors on the beach said, "What took you guys so long? You all swim like a bunch of old ladies." "Hoo-yah!" was the prompt reply from the students.

In the BUDS class that followed mine, at San Clemente Island, a student died on the five-and-a-half-mile swim. Hypothermia overtook him, and by the time he was unconscious, his body's inner-core temperature was eighty-two degrees. For hours, medical crews tried to revive him but could not. His name was John Tomlinson, and he was one incredibly dedicated SEAL trainee. The loss of his life hit all of us heavily, reminding us of the dangerous nature of SEAL training.

"Rock portage" was another dangerous set of Second Phase exercises. On the west side of San Clemente, the waves were usually high because of winter sea conditions. Rock portage involved landing our rafts on a rocky beach in the midst of the huge waves. The instructors intentionally waited until the waves were large before scheduling this activity so that we would learn how to negotiate treacherous beach conditions and get the "full benefit" of training. On the night selected by the instructors, the waves were enormous. The thundering crash of the surf zone resonated hundreds of yards away. Rock portage is among the most dangerous activities in SEAL training. If a man became trapped between the boat and a boulder, the moving raft was capable of snapping a leg with relative ease. Broken bones and lacerations could easily take place during this exercise.

From a calm harbor, our boat crew paddled northward out to sea to the area of the rock-landing site. A series of flashlight signals from shore directed us to begin paddling toward the rocks. Fortunately, increased visibility from a full moon and clear skies helped us to see some of the rocks on the beach and brace ourselves for oncoming waves. Moving closer to the rocks, I got a queasy feeling in my stomach as I thought of the awesome power of the waves. We paddled furiously, hoping to land on the rocks in a smaller set of waves and between the big breakers. Suddenly, I felt the undertow of a building wave that almost stopped all our forward motion. I knew that a wave was going to overtake us. As I turned my head to look behind us, the night sky disappeared behind a high wall of water. The next thing I knew, I was struggling to shore, hoping to reach a rock without being slammed against it. The boat had been flipped upside down with the squad members scattered about in the water. Eventually our boat crew reached the shore, and after several repetitions of the same activity, we were secured from rock portage. Being secured meant that we had successfully completed the drill and could return to the BUDS camp. Basically, the way to pass the test of rock portage was to stay out of the hospital.

After FTX maneuvers—the final missions on which our squads were evaluated—we had completed all of Second

Phase. The long month at San Clemente Island was over, and we packed our bags for the short flight home to Coronado for our third and final phase of training, Dive Phase. Leaving San Clemente, I felt numb to the world around me, sensing that I was capable of enduring nearly anything. Students at BUDS often said that guys coming home from San Clemente looked like SEALs because they looked weathered, serious, and ready to fight. Returning from the island, we did feel ready for anything. But with two more long months ahead, "the only easy day was yesterday."

7

DIVE PHASE

Scuba diving had always looked fun and exciting to me. After SEAL training, however, diving took on radically different connotations. Although combat diving was at times exciting, it was anything but fun. Combat-swimmer ship attacks are some of the most physically and mentally challenging operations that SEALs conduct. If there is one factor that separates SEALs from other Special Forces units, it is the SEALs' incredible underwater abilities and proficiency in the midst of the adverse nighttime oceans.

Third Phase, or Dive Phase, is extremely challenging for a variety of reasons. The required time limits for swims, runs, and obstacle courses were the fastest in BUDS and were also coupled with many rigorous mental tests and academic examinations. We were tested in physics, medicine, marine life, and numerous other subjects applying to the underwater world. Our physics exams required that we know algebra and trigonometry, as well as understand several laws relating to diving, compression of gases, and water displacement. Boyle's law, Charles's law, Dalton's law, and Archimedes' principle had to be learned, understood, and applied in mathematics exams. Enlisted men had to score above 80 percent on written exams, and officers were required to score 90 percent or higher. One or two students did not pass the physics exams and were disenrolled.

In addition to the physical and intellectual challenges of

Third Phase, we had to perform countless night and day dives. These underwater exercises required hours of planning subsurface approach routes to ships, tide-and-current calculations and corrections, total-time-of-dive estimates, and many other life-critical computations. Predive gear inspections were tedious, and attention to detail was crucial. After dives, cleaning and derigging our scuba and wet suits consumed much time and were exhausting.

Diving itself is one of the harshest physical activities in Third Phase, and during this phase we learned how to operate both open- and closed-circuit scuba. Open-circuit scuba (Self-Contained Underwater Breathing Apparatus) is simply air that has been compressed into tanks and is breathed into the lungs through a regulator and hose. The air is inhaled and exhaled, creating many bubbles that rise to the water's surface. Open-circuit scuba is what a great majority use for sport diving and is what most people are familiar with.

Closed-circuit scuba is different from open-circuit scuba. As the name implies, a closed-circuit breathing loop keeps all the oxygen inside the system. The oxygen travels from the tank into the lungs, out of the lungs through a separate hose into a chemical-scrubber canister, and then back into the lungs. Since the oxygen never escapes, there are no bubbles to rise to the water's surface. Because of the lack of telltale bubbles, a person on the surface of the water would never be aware of the closed-circuit divers unless the person visibly saw him.

The SEAL closed-circuit system, the German-made Draeger LAR V, is one of the SEAL's indispensable pieces of equipment. The Draeger uses pure oxygen rather than the compressed air of open-circuit systems. Breathing pure oxygen creates many complex hazards. First, inhaling pure oxygen below a twenty-five-foot depth for extended periods can cause a potentially fatal condition called oxygen toxicity. This toxicity arises from the raised partial pressure of oxygen in the body's blood stream. A second and common complication is called "Draeger ear." For some reason, using the pure-oxygen rig causes pain and popping in the inner ear, and this symptom is experienced several hours after the dive. A third hazard is carbon dioxide buildup. An improperly assembled rig can cause carbon dioxide levels to become high, which can cause dizziness, blurred vision, and blackouts.

The differences of difficulty between diving open- and closed-circuit scuba are like the difference between flying a kite and an airplane. Many Special Forces units steer away from the Draeger because of its complexities, and I have even over-heard other United States commandos refer to the Draeger as the "death rig." The inherent difficulties in using the Draeger are part of the reason for the tough academic standards and physics courses in BUDS.

Third Phase was tiring and stressful. Day and night dives, as well as rigorous cutoff times for runs, swims, and obstacle courses—in addition to intense math and physics exams—pushed all of us in ways that we had not yet been tested. Psychologically, Dive Phase forced us to develop a high level of mental control and coolheadedness in the midst of physical exhaustion. Diving closed-circuit scuba is fatiguing, cumbersome, restrictive, and dark. Most dives are conducted at night, the likely time for a SEAL platoon to infiltrate beneath a ship or pier. Darkness is one of the SEAL's greatest assets, as it provides a cloak to mask the movement of commandos. But darkness also adds barriers to technical operations such as diving. Even with glow-in-the-dark illumination, instruments such as depth and pressure gauges, watches, and compasses are difficult to read. What's more, orientation beneath dark water is drastically limited. The cold temperatures of Pacific diving cause limited dexterity, shivering, and cramps. Many compass bearings and distances must be memorized for swimming into the exact location of the target area, usually a ship. No written records can be kept on one's body during combat dives because of the risk of a swimmer pair (swim partners) being captured and the rest of the platoon being compromised. Those are just some of the many obstacles that night dives provide.

The physical stress of closed-circuit diving is also immense. Dives sometimes involve over one mile of swimming underwater at a greatly reduced pace. Currents and the weight of dive gear force swimmers to kick hard, steady strokes that burn out the thigh and hamstring muscles in the legs. Hours of kicking propel swimmer pairs into and out of ships, piers, and harbors-the areas that SEALs are likely to infiltrate on real missions.

Operating in the unnatural underwater environment also makes combat swimming difficult. Darkness underwater in murky ports is intimidating, making the experience uncomfortable and completely unnatural. The process of communication between a diver and his partner is also greatly limited. Systems of squeezes and a simple series of nudges allow combat swimmer pairs to send basic messages to one another. On many night dives our tide and current calculations were slightly off. That would result in our traveling to a different ship or even a different pier, as we had gently pushed off course during our infiltration to the target. The problem of finding out where we were and communicating that information to one another was further complicated because we were not allowed to break the water's surface to catch a peek if we

ARE THEY ALLOWED TO CARRY SMALL ERASABLE GREASE BOARDS?

HOW ABOUT A SMALL FLOATABLE GPS ANTENNA WITH A WIRE ATTACHED TO A HAND HELD RECEIVER?

were off target. Finding our bearing was difficult and called for ice-cold nerves and emotions. If the instructors, who were in boats on the surface, caught swimmer pairs taking peeks, the pair was pulled from the dive, punished, and given a failing grade for the dive. More than one such failure might result in disenrollment.

A test occurred in Dive Phase that continued to push aspiring SEALs to the limit. "Pool competency" was designed to evaluate a trainee's ability to think clearly and not panic while being "attacked" underwater. In this exercise, we were in the deep end of the pool and were breathing open-circuit scuba. SEAL instructors wearing fins and masks descended upon us, attacking us vigorously. Hoses were twisted, facemasks were pulled off, and air supplies were shut off. As we students attempted to fix our many complications so that we could breathe, the instructors wrestled us to the bottom of the pool. The test turned into a fight with the instructors as we struggled to maintain airflow from the scuba tanks. Grading depended on our ability to keep our composure and methodically prioritize and fix our scuba malfunctions. If a student panicked and bolted to the surface, he failed and had to repeat the procedure. Two candidates in my class were disenrolled, even after making it to Dive Phase.

As time passed slowly in Third Phase, the end of BUDS was now on the horizon. We became competent combat swimmers and learned the Draeger rig inside and out. Dive physics exams, pool competency, and tedious circumstances underwater molded us into the frame of the legendary Naval commandos. By the end of Dive Phase we were so adept at working underwater that we actually felt at home in the dark underwater world. The water became a refuge because it insulated us from the danger of being spotted. Later in the SEAL teams I came to appreciate more fully our underwater proficiency when, working with foreign Special Forces, we attempted to train them to perform the same diving operations that we did. It was impossible!

Graduation from BUDS drew near, and our class proctor, the instructor who helped us with administrative matters, called out our individual orders as we waited breathlessly to hear which new SEAL team would be ours.

There are three odd-numbered SEAL teams on the West Coast in Coronado (Seal Teams One, Three, and Five) and three even-numbered teams in Little Creek, Virginia (Two, Four, and Eight). Two Seal Delivery Vehicle (SDV) teams provide modern minisubmarines for extended underwater SEAL operations. One SDV team is located at Little Creek, and the other is stationed in Hawaii. Each SEAL team typically has six to eight platoons and each platoon has sixteen men. The SEAL platoon is the basic operating unit, and these platoons are stationed around the world, twenty-four hours a day, in case a response is needed to a sudden crisis. Different SEAL teams deploy to various geographical areas of operation. For example, Seal Team Five mostly deployed to Southeast Asia.

I still remember the proctor's words: "Air-man Watkins, SEAL Team Five, Coronado." I couldn't believe what the instructor had just said. A SEAL team actually wanted my abilities and skills. At that time, we were also issued orders to the United States Army's airborne course at Fort Benning, Georgia.

Graduation day was one of the mountaintop experiences of my life, and I was filled with an exhilarating sense of accomplishment. The ceremony was held on a perfect, sunny, San Diego morning at the Naval Amphibious Base in

Coronado, California. My father, mother, and sister were all there for the graduation, and I felt as if I could touch the clouds. As the Navy band played, the decorations on the instructors' dress uniforms sparkled in the Southern California sun. More than anyone else, I wanted my father to be proud of me on that day, and I know that he was. His approval was my greatest commendation.

PART THREE

INITIAL DEPLOYMENTS

8

CHARLIE PLATOON

Once I arrived at SEAL Team Five, I was assigned to Charlie Platoon, my first and longest experience as a fully qualified Navy SEAL. That platoon carried me to Southeast Asia, opening my eyes to fascinating parts of the world that I had never seen. But most important, it was in Charlie Platoon that God continued to draw me to Himself by His irresistible grace and save me for His sake. The most exciting part of Charlie Platoon was not the fast-paced SEAL operations, though they were exciting. The true thrill in my life came in the way God worked to open my eyes to my own sinfulness and rescue me from myself. Some Christians are saved through outwardly uneventful circumstances, but others, like me, God chooses to "hit over the head with a two-by-four." The most vivid event that I go back to when giving my Christian testimony occurred on an operation in Charlie Platoon, and it ended up nearly costing my life.

Training is the SEAL's daily job, and except for a few brief interruptions since the Vietnam War, SEALs continue to train round-the-clock. In Charlie Platoon, we learned desert, jungle, and arctic warfare tactics, as well as skills in advanced combat swimming, advanced medical training, hostage rescue missions, and a host of other special-warfare tasks. But coupled with long hard days of training was plenty of fun and time off. Unlike most other military units, SEALs are treated with much respect and compensation. Anytime we weren't training, our officers made sure that we received time off to take care of personal matters and enjoy sunny Southern California.

Living in an apartment on Coronado Island and going to work as a Navy SEAL should have been the "life of Riley." I had always thought that when I reached that point, I would find contentment in life. I had everything that I ever dreamed of in Charlie Platoon: a car that was paid for, a gorgeous apartment, a girlfriend, and at age nineteen, I was a point man in the first squad of a SEAL platoon. What I lacked, however, was peace, joy, and contentment. Contributing to my unrest was a fear of death and of what would happen to me if I died. I was also saturated with guilt over my sinful life. As a SEAL, my job failed to offer me an escape from thinking about dying. After all, dishing out death was the SEALs' specialty. But I kept attempting to drown my guilt with work and pleasure, both of which were plentiful.

OUR PLATOON PREPARES FOR THE PHILIPPINES

Charlie Platoon had twelve enlisted men and two officers (currently, SEAL platoons have fourteen enlisted men and two officers), and some members of my platoon were experience-hardened SEALs. Our training routine involved fast-paced advanced operations. Early on in the platoon I was a fairly decent marksman and eventually became qualified as the secondary sniper for the two-man platoon sniper team. A SEAL platoon is further divided into two squads. I was selected as the point man for the first squad, which meant that I navigated the squad's movement and conducted much of the scout reconnaissance for the platoon. In addition, I worked closely with the patrol leader, who was also the officer in charge of the platoon, a lieutenant in rank.

For over one year, our platoon trained for a six-month deployment to the Western Pacific region. Once deployed, we would be assigned to Naval Special Warfare Unit One in Subic Bay, the Philippines. From there we would be on call for any Seventh Fleet crisis or for a tasking from the Joint Special Operations Command. In preparation for our deployment to the Philippines, our platoon trained extensively in an assortment of commando skills. As the SEAL acronym implies, we must be prepared to strike a target anywhere on earth, sea, air, and land. Possessing this capability required expensive and exotic training conditions and wide-ranging travel.

Some of our special training and travel took place in Alaska, where the West Coast teams usually conduct winter warfare school. Charlie Platoon's deployment to Anchorage involved cold-weather training in which we learned some of the special skills needed to carry out assaults in extreme cold. The Navy bought us thousands of dollars' worth of gear to undergo the training. We also purchased some of our gear, such as boots, at a civilian sports store in San Diego. We joked with one another that receiving our expensive gear was like Christmas. If one were to look at our equipment, it would appear that we were a National Geographic expedition team.

There was a price to pay for all the fun and expensive gear. Arctic training was conducted under physically exhausting conditions and in environments that were naturally hostile and uncomfortable. The psychological edge of training was always the most difficult to maintain. Some of the missions that we were assigned to carry out seemed impossible at first consideration. But our "fire in the gut" and refusal to quit kept us going through miserable and dangerous operations.

It was February 1989 when Charlie Platoon deployed to Alaska. It just so happened that while we were there, a record cold front swept through, paralyzing much of Anchorage and other parts of the state. The record temperatures were dangerously low. We survived overnight without tents when the temperature was about forty degrees below zero. Digging "snow caves" in the sides of snow drifts, we were able to stay warm and endure the brutal cold. Survival alone is a difficult feat in those temperatures, but fighting in those conditions is nearly impossible. Weapons have to be lubricated with dry graphite compounds to prevent moving parts from freezing and thus from not functioning. Nothing metallic could be touched with bare skin because of what we called the "stick factor." Mobility, one of the SEALs' greatest assets, is greatly limited in the cold by heavy packs, snowshoes, and multilayered clothes. But as with every SEAL operation, we found ways to overcome and endure the circumstances and accomplish the mission. After operating in the miserable arctic conditions, I was ready to return to sunny Coronado, which seemed like a distant planet from the snow-covered peaks of the Alaskan mountains.

After returning to Coronado and receiving some time off after our training in Alaska, I became increasingly restless, not really knowing what to do with my free time. On SEAL operations, my mind was directly fixed on the mission, and there was little else to keep me preoccupied. But when I was on the beach or walking through beautiful Coronado, I constantly pondered the meaning of life and death. Incessant guilt finally prompted me to go to church in an attempt to deal with my questions and fears about death. Not knowing much about churches, creeds, or doctrinal distinctions, I went to a Baptist church on Coronado Island.

Following the service, I was approached by a cordial and sincere Sunday-school teacher named John Simpson. John introduced himself and invited me to his house for fellowship and Bible study during the week. He led a study with a group of civilians and Navy sailors from around the Coronado area. While I was visiting with John, he asked me why I had come to church. I replied that I was feeling guilty over the way I had been living and was scared that when I died, I would go to hell. John pointed me directly to the Bible, having a passage of Scripture to answer my every question. Confronted by the Bible verses, I quickly saw that I was not saved. I began attending home Bible studies with John and several other people at the church, along with some Navy guys who were stationed on aircraft carriers in Coronado. The more John taught the Bible, the clearer the issues became. The biblical message of salvation was this: to be saved, one must confess and repent of his sin, embrace Jesus Christ as Lord and Savior, and follow Him in obedience. After hours of listening to John, I was still not ready to commit my life to Christ. I wanted security, but I was not yet desperate enough to change my way of living, as Jesus had clearly commanded His followers to do.

Charlie Platoon continued to train hard in preparing for deployment to the Philippines, but my involvement with John's Bible study faded and became nonexistent. Learning advanced SEAL skills as a qualified operator lifted me to new heights of achievement. I was proud of my platoon and of my status as a SEAL. Walking with Charlie Platoon across a runway to board an aircraft for a parachute operation was simply uplifting. Carrying exotic weapons and wearing wet suits, parachutes, and camouflage face paint, our platoon attracted attention at the airfield. The thought overwhelmed me that I was no longer an aspiring SEAL; I was a United States Navy SEAL.

The day of our deployment drew near, and our platoon became sharper and sharper as a team. Firing a variety of weapons and learning to negotiate any terrain, we honed our vital commando skills. Compared with training in the Teams, BUDS was called "basic" for a good reason. At Team Five, each individual in the platoon was trained as an independent leader, capable of commanding a SEAL patrol should the ranking leaders become disabled on a mission. A key in all the platoon training was to develop the ability to think critically under pressure and to evaluate complex scenarios in a fast, efficient, and calm manner. Every facet of training was designed to produce the operator's ability to control the situation, no matter how desperate it became.

GOD SPARES MY LIFE

God began to show me who was really in control of my life at this time during platoon training. Our platoon was preparing for a special mission called Combat Search and Rescue (CSAR). On that mission, a SEAL patrol would infiltrate, locate, and recover a downed pilot who had survived ejection or crash landing behind enemy lines. On San Clemente Island, the same island on which the Second Phase of BUDS was conducted, we rehearsed for the CSAR operation. Returning to the island felt strange to me, as I remembered the torturous circumstances of Second Phase. This time, however, I was there to carry out a professional training mission and not to be harassed.

Our objective was to travel in a <u>combat</u> rubber raiding craft to a beach on the southwest side of San Clemente Island,

EVERYTHING IS COMBAT THIS AND COMBAT THAT,

send swimmer scouts to shore, and then locate a suitable landing beach for the boat. Then we would patrol to the pilot and extract him. After extracting, we would make our way back out through the surf zone to rendezvous with a Naval patrol boat. What was an ordinarily routine mission turned into a nightmare that nearly claimed my life. The reason for the precarious situation was a surf zone that contained eight- to twelve-foot-high plunging waves and a rocky coastline shrouded in a dark mist.

I ended up as the driver and steered the fifty-five-horsepower Johnson outboard motor. On the mission, it was my turn to gain experience and proficiency in boat handling. Our infiltration took place at about 1:00 A.M. as we launched our two swimmer scouts. The scouts swam onto the beach, reconnoitering the area for a suitable landing spot. The plan followed that, once a suitable landing point was found, the swimmers would signal our patrol with a subtle red-lens flashlight. I would then steer the boat to shore. After waiting a long time for the scouts to reply, we saw a signal from the beach, a red-flashing light. As we made our approach to the surf zone, it became obvious that the waves were going to be large because of the rising and falling swells.

The scouts had made a mistake. While they were climbing up and down a treacherous section of rocks along the base of a cliff, the red-lens flash-light was inadvertently activated, giving us a false signal. The scouts had never intended to call us in on the location that we were rapidly approaching. As the scouts heard our engines coming, they screamed to abort the landing, but the thundering breakers drowned their voices out. Because of the heavy marine layer of fog, we could not see the rocky shoreline. I sensed trouble when the under-tow of a huge wave began to bog down the engine. Suddenly, darkness overtook us as a plunging wave turned our boat upside down, scattering our patrol in all directions. We were hit in our heads with weapons and held underwater for a seeming eternity.

Crashing against the rocks, we struggled to grab hold of a secure position and climb out of the crushing surf. I had some mild lacerations, bruises, and was shaken up, but managed to make my way to the rest of the patrol, all of whom were in a similar condition. After our platoon had regrouped, the patrol leader made the decision to go back out through the surf zone and then land again on a softer beach. The most surprising part of the plan was that the outboard motor restarted after being slammed against the rocks and held underwater for several minutes. During this first landing, the second squad was in a separate boat, beyond the surf, and was waiting for our radio call to make an approach.

I steered the boat as we made an attempt to break out through the vicious waves. A huge wave was building, and as we approached its base, the boat had reached full speed. The result was a disaster, for we hit the "plunger" head on. I saw everyone jump out and away from the heavy raft so as not to get pinned under the capsizing boat. However, I could not jump right or left as I attempted to steer the engine, which was still running at full throttle. The raft went up the oncoming wave, stood straight on its end, and then the bow came up, over, and back onto me as it flipped upside down. I was unable to escape from under the boat and ended up being pinned beneath the raft, which weighed about a thousand pounds. Making matters worse, a piece of my gear was evidently caught on the motor. I was quickly running out of air as I fought furiously to get loose from the boat. Using all my strength to try to free myself caused me to use even greater amounts of oxygen. After nearly two minutes of struggling underwater without a breath, I was nearing unconsciousness. The world seemed to stand still as I realized that death was overtaking me. The only thought that filled my mind was what the newspapers would say about my death. I feared that my life would be viewed as a tragic and needless loss. Now, there was no remaining energy with which to fight.

What little sense of feeling remained in my limbs was stimulated when a hand grabbed my wrist. Symbolically, it was the hand of God sparing my life. In reality God was using the hand of my platoon commander, Lt. Steve Simmet. Steve had noticed that I was not on the surface and began swimming under the capsized raft to try to find me. He was successful in untangling my hung body and managed to work me safely to the surface. Once the night air hit my face, I took deep inhalations of air, which burned my lungs as I coughed up salt water. My legs felt like they weighed a thousand pounds, and I couldn't even move them since I was weak from lack of oxygen.

I had the presence of mind to pull the actuator that inflated my UDT life jacket. Just when the life jacket filled with carbon dioxide, a huge plunging wave crashed on Steve and me, separating us on impact. Nearly passing out a second time, I was tossed about underwater. Eventually, a wave slammed me onto a coastal rock, which I managed to cling to in an effort to stay on shore. Landing on the boulder split open my shin, but I managed to pull myself to higher ground before another huge set of waves could sweep me back into the black sea.

Pulling myself to a standing position, I looked for other members of the patrol. A bandanna was useful as a makeshift bandage for my shin. Within ten to fifteen minutes our patrol had re-grouped. None of us was badly hurt, and we worked together to move the beached raft onto the rocks. The engine was completely broken this time, and there was no hope of restarting it.

Lieutenant Simmet organized our platoon and directed me, the point man, to patrol to the location of the downed pilot. At that point, it occurred to me that nothing short of paralysis or death would stop a SEAL patrol from reaching their objective. After recovering the pilot, we called in the second raft on a calmer beach. Hooking up a towline from the second raft to the downed raft, we were successful in pulling the broken raft back out through the surf zone. We were then able to extract to the pickup boats about one mile offshore. While we watched from there, the naval gunboats opened fire, raking the beach with an assortment of armaments.

That night, I knew God had spared my life. It was as if He had spoken directly to me through the "accident" in the raft. From that point onward, I began carefully reading the Bible, and I even returned to John's Bible-study group to ask more questions about salvation. But our deployment for six months to the Philippines was now only weeks away. John encouraged me to read a book called The Gospel According to Jesus by John MacArthur, Jr., who is a pastor in Southern California. I threw the book in my gear, which was in the process of being packed for the deployment. I could hardly wait to deploy overseas with the platoon. As I set out for the Philippines with excitement over the adventures and missions awaiting me, God planned to teach me that the most dangerous way to live life is by disobeying His will.

9

SAVED IN A STRANGE COUNTRY

Arriving in the Philippines thrilled me since it was my first overseas adventure. The lush green jungles surrounding the Subic Bay naval base were mesmerizing. Gazing out the window of the bus on the ride from the airfield, I could hardly wait to get out into the towns and provinces and explore the exotic new land. But first, we had to unpack, pass customs, receive our intelligence briefings, and tend to many other administrative and logistical matters. After all those tedious details were finished, we were then allowed off-base privileges and could venture out into the Philippine culture.

Nearly as fast as our bags were unpacked, our platoon was put on a flight to Guam to train for a special mission. The mission involved sliding down special ropes, called "fast ropes," from a helicopter onto the deck of a moving ship. The operation was difficult, requiring excellent pilots who could hold a steady hover that matched the speed of the moving tanker. While the helicopter was above the moving ship, the fast ropes were thrown to the deck of the tanker and then the platoon would quickly slide down the ropes. Practicing constantly, the platoon finally accomplished the delivery of fourteen SEALs from the helicopter to the deck of the moving ship in less than twenty seconds. It was an impressive spectacle, and one that was incredibly dangerous, even in training.

There was a motto in the Teams that said, "Work hard, play hard." While in Guam and during weekend breaks from stressful training, the platoon usually headed into town to "cut loose." I went out with the platoon a number of times, but I became increasingly convicted over my sin and kept thinking about John's warnings to repent. I couldn't have fun with the platoon anymore because of the weight of guilt that God was pressing upon me. Reading the Bible with an ever-increasing curiosity about Jesus and salvation, I had reached the point where I knew that my commitment had to be either to this world and my sin, or to Jesus Christ. To receive and follow Christ as Lord and Savior, I would need to repent of my sin, ask for forgiveness, and trust in Jesus' sacrificial death. Nothing could have been clearer from an intellectual standpoint. But I knew that embracing Christ would result in separation from the platoon and times of loneliness for myself.

One morning, as our platoon rehearsed the dangerous ship-boarding maneuver, God used the "final straw" to draw me to Himself. The helicopter raced toward the moving tanker at over a hundred miles per hour while we prepared to board the vessel. Platoon members braced themselves with bent knees, ready to slide down the thick fast-rope. Suddenly, the helicopter began to shake violently. The pilot's overcompensated pull on the controls caused the chopper to rise above the moving ship's smokestacks. The CH-46 helicopter began what is called Pilot-Induced Oscillation (PIO), in which the aircraft's computer automatically overrides the pilot from making radically dangerous maneuvers. The battle between the pilot and the computer override caused the helicopter to shake violently and slide toward the ship's smokestacks. The pilot eventually recovered control and aborted the pass at the last second. After the mission debriefing, the crew chief, who had been a Navy aircrewman for over twenty years, said that he had survived two previous helicopter crashes. But when this PIO incident took place, he didn't expect to live through it. A sick feeling overtook me as my mind jumped immediately to the entrapment under the raft less than one month earlier.

Returning to the barracks in Guam, I finally yielded to the conviction of God over my sin. I realized that I deserved eternal punishment for my sins and that my only hope of being reconciled to God was by submitting to Jesus as Lord and Savior. I knew that only Jesus, through His perfect and sinless life, death, and resurrection, could satisfy God's justice and atone for my sins. Asking God to forgive me of my sins and expressing in prayer that I wanted to follow Jesus Christ for the rest of my life, I committed my life to Him. At that point, I truly didn't want to sin anymore.

Following Jesus involves obedience to His commands in Scripture. Jesus said, "He who has My commandments and keeps them, he it is who loves Me; and he who loves Me shall be loved by My Father, and I will love Him, and will disclose Myself to him (John 14:21)." My commitment to follow Christ caused the rest of the platoon, none of whom were Christians, to be in immediate opposition to me. They thought I had lost my mind and wondered why I would not run with them in fleshly pursuits. When I refused to go along with them to bars and houses of ill repute, they tried to make me feel guilty for not being "one of the boys."

Looking back on the experience now, I believe they knew that what they were doing was immoral and were convicted by my stand for Christ. They tried to get me to indulge with them because my life of abstinence was a constant reminder to them of their own sinful behavior. Their reaction was exactly as the Bible said it would be: "They [unbelievers] are surprised that you do not run with them into the same excess of dissipation, and they malign you (1 Peter 4:4)."

Returning to the Philippines after the fast-paced training in Guam was tough for me. The majority of the activities off base were immoral and spiritually damaging, especially for a new Christian. I began a physical workout that was more intense than ever, as I found it to be an effective way for venting my frustrations and fighting the ever present temptations of Olongapo City. I also spent many lonely nights in my barracks reading Scripture while the rest of the platoon usually indulged in activities that I could not even allow myself to think about. But God allowed me to grow spiritually strong during that time, and He rewarded me by granting new friends who were more than just friends—they were brothers and sisters in Christ. I also learned to rely on Him fully for strength and daily courage in living a new life for my Savior.

A Navy friend and brother in Christ named Dave Votroubek wrote to me from California, where he was stationed. He was involved with John Simpson's Bible-study group in Coronado and recommended a church near the naval base in the Philippines. With the church's address in hand, I headed off the naval base and ventured into Olongapo City to find the First Olongapo Fundamental Baptist Church (FOFBC). FOFBC is a Filipino church, but the sermons were delivered by Pastor Henry Senina in English. There were usually only one or two Americans per service. Discovering a new family of Christians was intimidating at first because I wasn't exactly sure how to act and was afraid that I would violate some code of behavior. The family of believers at FOFBC was overwhelmingly gracious and loving as they demonstrated the true spirit of the Lord, who governed their hearts and minds. I was welcomed with open and generous arms.

Pastor Henry Senina and his family, along with countless other Christians at FOFBC, taught me, by words and deeds, what it meant to be saved. In the midst of poverty and incredible hardships, the people at the church had a love and joy for serving Christ that was infectious. I don't think the word complaint was in their vocabulary. No matter how adverse their situations were, they continued to praise God and give Him thanks for all His blessings. The flock at FOFBC demonstrated the spirit of sharing in ways that only Jesus can fully produce. Families in the Philippines often had no idea where their next meal would come from. However, at meal times, anyone who was in their presence was offered an equal or greater portion of what everyone else was eating. I remember thinking that the churches in the United States could be taught some valuable lessons about Christlikeness from our Filipino brothers and sisters.

A beautiful aspect of worshipping God with the believers in the Philippines was our unity in Christ. Although we were culturally and ethnically oceans apart, we had strong unconditional love for one another. That is what the Bible calls "agape" love, and it comes only through knowing Christ Jesus as Lord and Savior. I made special friends at FOFBC, and Pastor Henry will always remind me of an ideal pastor because he led God's flock by example. God used those saints to overcompensate for the lonely isolation I felt from my platoon.

Members of Charlie Platoon treated me differently on an individual level. Some acted in an openly hostile fashion while others just wrote my conversion off as a "religious phase." They all agreed, however, that I had undergone a change. At the same time, they increased the pressure on me to run with them in their drinking and carousing on weekends.

THE PUREST LOVE: LOVE NOT ADULTERATED BY SEX

I thought it was strange that I was criticized for being a Christian, but was invited to go to the bars with them. God taught me not to take it personally because I knew that it was the old Steve they wanted to see. What they didn't like in me was really Jesus Christ.

After my conversion, I wrestled with some common arguments that unbelievers use against Christians to attack their faith. For example, I was deeply convicted over my own sin, but unbelievers say that such conviction isn't from God. Rather, they say it comes from society's old-fashioned ideas about morality and is a result of years of cultural mores and folkways that condition one to feel guilty. According to their viewpoints, one should not feel guilty at all.

But such reasoning is flawed for several reasons. First, I was never indoctrinated with puritanical sets of rules in my upbringing, and the "watered-down" churches that I had attended had adopted a moral relativism where situation ethics reigned and the distinction between right and wrong was blurred. Second, in Charlie Platoon I was in the midst of one of the most sin-tolerant and sin-accepting cities known to man-Olongapo. Sinning with the SEAL platoon not only was normal and accepted, but was even encouraged and touted as a virtue. In the Philippines, immorality was both for sale and legal. So if ever there could be a place where the conscience was loosed from cultural and societal restraint, it was in Olongapo. In spite of all the immoral encouragement and urging of my peers, God had convicted my heart more than ever, and that pain was very real.

John MacArthur's book The Gospel According to Jesus helped lay open the Word of God in a way clear and consistent with what I read in the Scriptures. His thesis in that book is the answer to a question that appears as a caption on the book's cover: "What does Jesus mean when He says, 'Follow Me'?" I quickly understood that following Christ meant that an individual must submit himself in obedience to His will, and that even submission was wholly a work of His grace. One had to abandon his own desires and cast himself at the feet of Jesus, pleading for the forgiveness of his sins. God forgives repentant sinners by His free grace on the basis of Christ's atoning work on the cross.

JOHN 6:65

Although my platoon harassed me because of my Christian faith, they did respect my professional abilities as a SEAL. God granted me the ability to excel at marksmanship and become one of two platoon snipers. He also granted proficiency and competency as a SEAL operator, allowing me to gain the respect of the more experienced SEALs in the platoon. Even though they ridiculed my faith, they couldn't help but respect me in the realm of SEAL operations. They also knew that I would have laid down my life for them, and they had to at least give me some credit for that.

Charlie Platoon continued to train hard. We patrolled in the jungles, parachuted, and prepared for hostage rescue missions called "close-quarters battle (CQB)." Charlie Platoon earned the Meritorious Unit Commendation for missions aboard a nuclear submarine while practicing clandestine infiltration off the South Korean coast. We traveled to Guam and the Marshall Islands numerous times to rehearse rapid-deployment operations. As a platoon, we worked in orchestral fashion coordinating complex operations under stress. I learned nearly every trick in the book when it came to shooting, diving, parachuting, and a host of other SEAL skills.

Things heated up in December 1989. Only weeks before the United States "Just Cause" invasion of Panama, a military coup d'état took place in the Philippines. President Corazon

Aquino's army split into two factions, and most Philippine Special Forces units aligned themselves with the rebel cause. That made for some tense moments between the United States Navy and factions of the Philippine military, some of which were stationed at Subic Bay. President George Bush supported Aquino, and United States fighter aircraft from Clark Air Base flew low-level intimidation passes over many air bases in an effort to ground Philippine planes. A coordinated muscle-flex by the United States turned the tide of the coup, giving the rebels the clear message that if they continued to overthrow Aquino, they would have to take on the United States. Aquino prevailed, and fortunately there was little bloodshed, and there were no American casualties.

Every time our platoon received liberty in Subic Bay, I went to the FOFBC worship services. I grew close to the brothers and sisters there, and they encouraged and discipled me as a new believer. Pastor Henry was especially encouraging to me. His selfless devotion to the people of the church was an example of the Christlikeness in him. Soft-spoken and humble, Pastor Henry prayed with me and even asked me to speak to the church one Sunday evening. That was a tremendous thrill, as Pastor Henry, more than anyone else, was used by God to stimulate my desire for the ministry in years to come.

During the six-month deployment to the Philippines with Charlie Platoon, I not only received salvation, but also grew close to the Lord, learning to rely on Him for everything. When I was alone, my thoughts pondered how lonely Jesus must have been on many nights when He retreated to the Mount of Olives to pray to His Father. Knowing that "we [Christians] do not have a high priest who cannot sympathize with our weaknesses, but one [Christ] who has been tempted in all things as we are, yet without sin (Hebrews 4:15)," gave me strength when I was isolated and made fun of by the platoon. At the same time, God blessed me with many new brothers and sisters in Christ who were, and continue to be, a heartwarming support.

God also granted me abilities as a SEAL that earned the respect of my fellow soldiers, even when they were at odds with my Savior. In the Philippines, I had little grasp of the great things that lay ahead. The Lord was preparing me to be used by Him in amazing ways. He was going to not only send me behind enemy lines as a SEAL, but also use my Christian testimony as a witness to other SEALs who would later come to know Christ as their Lord and Savior. Just when we least expect it, God uses us for His glory in ways we have never dreamed of. My new life and adventures had only just begun.

10.

FOXTROT PLATOON

Returning to the United States after a six-month deployment was wonderful. I learned to truly appreciate how great America is through an extended separation. In January 1990, Charlie Platoon was disbanded; some of us were reassigned, while others were transferred to other SEAL teams. Five of us stayed together and were reassigned to Foxtrot Platoon, which had just been formed. I was enthusiastic about having a new platoon and didn't know at that time that the accomplishments of my new platoon would become well known in the SEAL community and in the national media.

The first training operation I embarked upon with Foxtrot involved marksmanship and small-arms proficiency in the mountains of Southern California. Five men who had just graduated from airborne school, and BUDS before that, also joined Foxtrot Platoon as new members, and they were fired up and motivated. They all had great attitudes, and their zeal was infectious to me as we traveled to the mountain shooting range. It was not yet clear who our platoon commander would be, but from the very start I saw Foxtrot Platoon as full of talent and positive attitudes. We fired MP-5 nine-millimeter submachine guns and Sig Sauer nine-millimeter pistols to refine and maintain weapons proficiency. Snow began to fall in the mountains as we fired our weapons, and having lived six months in Southeast Asia, the snow added a homey feeling to the outing.

In between volleys of fire, Lt. Tom Deitz appeared at the shooting range. Deitz had an air of success about him, and when our platoon found out that he might be our new officer-in-charge, we all hoped he would be selected. Deitz was one of those rare individuals who had all the right mix of qualities to be not only a military leader, but also a natural SEAL Team leader. He was liked by everyone in the platoon instantly. A graduate of the United States Naval Academy at Annapolis, he was a superior athlete, talented leader, and was sharp mentally and intellectually. He possessed the personal skills of a diplomat and was capable of putting an otherwise tense platoon at ease with a few soft words. A couple weeks later, word was out that Lieutenant Deitz had been selected as the new platoon commander of Foxtrot. The platoon couldn't have been happier, and at that time I sensed we were capable of accomplishing great things.

Our training took us to various locations. One was Niland, California, the training site of the West Coast SEAL teams. Camp Billy Machen is located on a large naval gunnery range in the Imperial Valley desert, where operations ranging from desert warfare to demolitions and explosives are conducted. Niland was also the sight of land navigation training and close-quarters battle. Foxtrot performed extremely well and breezed through the initial platoon land-warfare training course, which was graded and evaluated by senior trainers.

We also trained in the SEAL winter warfare school on Kodiak Island, Alaska, where I experienced the coldest moment of my life. As an initiation into the school, the platoon traveled to a cove on the coast of the island where a pier jutted out into the icy ocean. From the pier, we were required to strip down to our swim trunks and then take a five-minute plunge into the water. The water temperature was thirty degrees. At that temperature, fresh water would have normally been frozen; however, the salt content prevented the ocean water from freezing. When we first entered the water, a burning sensation covered our skin. The water touching our bare skin was literally colder than ice. Eventually the stinging sensation went away as our nerves became numb. Dexterity had almost vanished as we clumsily pulled ourselves back onto the pier. We shivered our way to the warm bus, and warmth slowly returned to our bodies on the ride back to the barracks.

No one seemed to know why we were put through that miserable experience. We were told that the "cold-water exposure" was designed to demonstrate the importance of wearing a dry suit during water transport in the frigid waters. Dry suits were worn during cold-water operations, and the suits perform their function by keeping water separated from the skin. Dry suits are much warmer than wet suits, but none of us needed any motivation to wear dry suits. We were quite aware of the dangers of cold-water exposure and hypothermia. Later we joked about the whole experience. One person in the platoon sarcastically said, "They might as well shoot us to teach us the importance of wearing body armor!"

Placing Mines on Ship Hulls

Another area of specialized training presented unique and challenging obstacles to our platoon: the combat swimmer course in Bangor, Washington, just south of Seattle. Combat swimmer courses enabled us to practice long underwater infiltrations, which were designed for attacking naval vessels in port. This involved placing limpet mines on the ship hulls of docked naval combatants. The water temperature in the

Puget Sound averaged forty-eight degrees during our training. The course was extremely challenging, and I found combat swimming to be one of the most mentally and physically demanding of all the SEAL missions. One particular combat ship-attack in Bangor serves as an appropriate example of the challenges we faced.

For our practice in placing limpet mines on the ship hulls, we used an old mothballed fleet of ships at the Puget Sound Naval Shipyard in Bremerton, near Bangor. Our target was a United States aircraft carrier, the USS Coral Sea, which had fought in legendary battles in the South Pacific. The decommissioned ship was a shadow of its former self, sitting peacefully in the lonely harbor at the naval base. The water was a cold fifty degrees, and at 11:00 P.M. there was little ambient light because of an abundance of cloud cover. Our mission was standard: infiltrate over one mile underwater; locate the Coral Sea; plant a limpet mine on the port, stern, and aft of the struts; then swim our one-thousand-meter exfiltration leg, and extract in a rubber raft.

The hum of the two-cycle outboard engines added to the tensions of the night air while we headed toward our insertion point. As the Boston Whaler glided across the icy waters of the Puget Sound, my dive partner, Mark, was visibly nervous. This was his first combat dive of this caliber, and we were being graded on our performance for this exercise. Each pair received a grade that applied to both divers. A failing grade for this Final Training Exercise could lead to disqualification as SEAL combat swimmers, so there was no room for error. Since Mark was new to the SEAL teams and this was his first exposure to a combat swimmer course, he knew that he was being especially scrutinized for any signs of deficiency by the trainers of our SEAL team.

Steve Watkins during "Hell Week"
Coronado, California

First Squad of Foxtrot — Saudi Arabia
Tom Deitz (standing center) Steve Watkins (standing far R)

Mike Bailey, Eric Hatter, & Steve Watkins
Malaysia, 1991

Pastor Henry Senina baptizing Eric Hatter

Steve Watkins
Philippines, 1991

Green Berets — Fort Bragg

Steve Watkins (L) with champion fighter Rickson Gracie (R) and his son Rockson,

Practicing Shipboarding off Guam

Steve Watkins — Kenton Baptist Church
Kenton, Kentucky, 2004

Foxtrot Platoon — Saudi Arabia
Operation Desert Storm, 1991

Mark and I had rehearsed this dive at length. We planned a solution to every conceivable problem that could have arisen. It was now 11:50 P.M., and in ten minutes we would be submerged in the fifty-degree water, heading into the blackness toward the Coral Sea. Our equipment had been inspected, our explosive mines had been safety checked, and our heads were clear. "Are you ready?" were my last words to him before we spent the next three hours underwater. Mark answered with a thumbs-up.

The water was so cold upon initial entry that it caused a sharp headache. As we kicked our fins, water seeped into every last part of our wet suits. The only thing visible was a greenish glow emanating from the different depth and scuba gauges. I could not see Mark, but a squeeze on my elbow every minute informed me that he was OK. After we had swum for over an hour, the compass that guided us began to spin in circles, indicating a metallic object, and I thought that we were nearing the USS Coral Sea. I kept swimming, trying to maintain a straight course, when my head struck the side of a ship. The force of the hit jarred my face mask loose, causing a stream of water to flood my face. As I cleared the water from my mask, Mark squeezed out a signal on my arm, asking what was going on. It was pitch-black, and we could not even see each other's face. I gave Mark the signal that I was OK and headed toward the aft of the ship.

As we approached the ship's rear, we hit a metal barrier that had not been anticipated. This threw all my estimates into confusion. Where were we? I started to second guess that we were in fact at the Coral Sea. We could not descend any further because our pure-oxygen scuba systems limited our depth to twenty-five feet. After deciding there were no other options, we began to make an ascent to the surface, hoping to see where we were. As our depth decreased slowly, we neared the surface. At five feet below sea level, we hit a steel surface above us. I could not believe what was happening. We appeared to be trapped with metal on all directions, except below us. Our oxygen supply gauge indicated about one hour of breathing time left. Because of the blackness, my sense of feel was all that I had to go by. Panic was an enemy at this point as I tried to think and remain composed. I remembered that ships are welded together with seams that could be felt with the hands. I then attempted to find a horizontal weld seam. Following the seam in either direction would eventually lead me out to the end of the ship since the seams run horizontally for the entire length of the ship.

After going back and forth on the ship with my hand, I finally hit a weld seam. Following the weld seam for over one minute, we finally reached one end of the carrier, and the water lightened up just enough to see the silhouette of Mark's body. Because there were no propellers, I determined that we were on the bow of the ship. We proceeded to swim away from the ship in a box-shaped pattern. In this maneuver, we were trained to swim straight away from the ship for a distance and then turn at right- or left-handed angles so that we would come back into the same ship, further toward the bow or stern. The technique worked, and we found the stern of the ship and planted our limpet mine. It turned out that we had hit the ship at an unestimated spot where a submarine had been moored to the aircraft carrier. We had managed to swim underwater to the point where the two combatants touched one another. But underwater, in the pitch-black ocean, the two vessels seemed to us like only a maze of steel and confusion.

There was not much oxygen remaining in our rigs, so we had to swim as fast as we could to get away from the ship before surfacing. As we pushed off from the massive carrier, we began kicking vigorously. We were able to swim at least four hundred yards before I began having difficulty breathing, which was a signal that my rig was running out of oxygen. Finally, we made our ascent and continued to swim the extraction distance. After a few hundred yards of swimming on the surface, we reached the extraction boat.

After the cold, miserable combat swimmer training, sunny Coronado was always a great place to unwind and relax from the frigid waters of the Puget Sound and Kodiak Island. We went back to Niland, California, to rehearse close-quarters battle, room takedowns, and other advanced skills. Our platoon functioned and performed well together, having all the right combinations of personality for success. With Lieutenant Deitz leading us, there didn't seem to be anything too challenging for us.

Our scheduled deployment to the Philippines was set for October, and as that date approached, our platoon continued to train and prepare for the trip assignment. One remaining course of training was "advanced land war-fare." That training involves the polishing of basic land-warfare skills and also incorporates more difficult exercises, including increasingly dangerous live-fire maneuvers. Our drills with live ammunition were a rare method for peacetime military units. Foxtrot Platoon was scheduled to conduct advanced land warfare in Montana, near Helena.

ATTENDING SNIPER SCHOOL WITH GREEN BERETS

Just prior to the deployment to Montana, Bruce Larson, our first-squad radioman, and I were selected to attend an advanced sniper school at Fort Bragg, North Carolina. Since

Bruce and I had already been chosen as the two primary platoon snipers and had previously completed SEAL sniper courses, Lieutenant Deitz wanted us to have broader exposure to other Special Forces sniper training. So Bruce and I received orders to Special Operations Target Interdiction Course (SOTIC) at the home of the Green Beret's training compound, the John F. Kennedy Special Warfare Center, Fort Bragg. We began preparing for sniper school as the rest of Foxtrot Platoon packed their bags for Montana. Since Bruce and I had both completed advanced land warfare, Lieutenant Deitz pulled the necessary strings so that we could skip the Montana trip and go directly to Fort Bragg.

Driving in the early morning hours to a private rifle range in the foothills east of San Diego, Bruce and I trained hard everyday to prepare for sniper school. We shot M-14 rifles with iron sights from the prone position. Our preference for firing the heavy M-14s was because of their relatively heavy trigger that forced us to develop a smooth and steady control of the trigger, a valuable tool for accurate marksmanship. I even quit drinking coffee, a monumental sacrifice for me, to try to further calm my nerves.

Our preparations also included the making of two Ghuille suits (pronounced gil-lee). Ghuille suits are made of shredded burlap strands sewn to camouflage fatigues, which have canvass-reinforced sections on the front of the shirt and thigh areas of the pants. The heavy canvass makes contact with the ground when a sniper is in the process of stalking and crawling. The suits made us look like Bigfoot. When a Ghuille-clad sniper is lying flat on the ground in high grass and shrubs, it is almost impossible to see him. These suits take hours to construct, and I used all my sewing skills that I had received at parachute rigger's school in custom-making the outfits. Bruce and I tried to document the number of hours spent working on the suits, but we soon gave up since it seemed to require countless hours of shredding, shopping, sewing, searching for pieces of hardware, and doing various other tedious preparations. Three weeks of working on the suits and shooting hundreds of 7.62-millimeter bullets thoroughly prepared us for the trip to Fort Bragg.

The look on the Green Berets' faces was unforgettable when Bruce and I pulled up to the sniper school in our rented Lincoln Town Car. The SEAL teams had sent us on a commercial airline, put us up in an off-base hotel in Fayetteville, North Carolina, and had rented us a car for commuting between the sniper school and hotel. All the Green Berets arrived together in an olive drab-green Army truck and were wearing camouflage fatigue uniforms. We pulled up in a white Lincoln, wearing blue jeans, polo shirts, and badly needing haircuts according to Army standards. Rarely did West Coast SEALs attend SOTIC, and the Green Berets were not used to the laid-back ways of Southern California SEAL teams. The sight of Bruce and me was foreign to the regimented Army Special Forces.

Actually, SEAL Team Five had rented us an economy car, and the rental company had guaranteed us budget rates. However, since all the company's economy cars had been rented at the time of our arrival, they gave us the Lincoln and charged us the reduced price. We didn't complain and always looked forward to our luxurious morning and evening rides to and from Mott Lake, the Fort Bragg site of SOTIC. The Army and Navy are two different organisms indeed, and the SEALs are as different from Green Berets as water is from dry land, even though we both share some of the same unconventional tactics and strategies in combat.

(handwritten margin note, rotated): 1" AT 25 YDS, NO SCOPE! 1" IS IN 2 LITER BOTTLE CAP SIZE

More than anything else, sniper school was mentally challenging. The first test we faced, on the morning of day one, was a qualification shoot. At twenty-five yards, we were required to shoot six groups of three bullets from the prone position. The targets were six small circles measuring one inch in diameter. To pass the test we had to place all eighteen bullets within the six circles, three bullets in each circle. A bullet hole outside a circle would disqualify a student and result in his dismissal from sniper school. That the rifles were fitted with iron sights (i.e., no telescopic sights) made the task of hitting the target even more difficult. Even one small slip of the finger was enough to cause us to be disenrolled from training. Bruce and I passed the test, but we both lost a little sweat in the process.

The next two weeks were filled with daily practical shoots and classroom instruction in subjects such as camouflage; tracking; advanced clandestine infiltration; ballistics; bullet reloading; mathematical calculations for wind, distance, and climate; and advanced reconnaissance techniques. We loved every minute of the course and thrived on the classes as knowledgeable Green Beret instructors shared volumes of information on the art of sniping. Bruce and I improved our marksmanship skills, especially our ability to hit difficult targets. Difficult targets generally result from a combination of unpredictable factors like distance (over eight hundred yards), movement (such as a motorcade), and limited visibility because of darkness, or a small target that moves randomly in front of an exposed space.

The theme of the course was simple, but challenging: "Make one shot equal one kill, undetected." Sniping is a cool, calculated art and has been a common tactic historically in both conventional and unconventional warfare. Sniping is also viewed by most conventional military leaders as a "dirty" type of warfare, as if charging a machine-gun nest was "clean" warfare. Since sniper employment is viewed as dark and sinister work, rarely, if ever, do commissioned officers attend military sniper courses. The military is still tied to the age-old chivalrous tradition of "an officer and a gentleman."

Bruce and I were anything but chivalrous, and although it may sound paradoxical, our hearts sympathized somewhat for conventional infantry-men (called grunts) who might have to face us in war. They would never see or hear us when we would engage them in a one-sided battle. But the unconventional way of fighting made more sense to us than did charging machine-gun nests. The ethos of most SEALs was to make the enemy give his life for his country, not the other way around. And if that required the employment of so-called "dirty" tactics, so be it.

The first requirement for becoming a sniper is an intense desire to be one. Patience and a steady trigger-finger are the chief qualities that must be mastered in sniper school, with patience being the element most needed for extended stalks. Stalks are field operations designed to test our ability to approach a target, make a shot, and then exfiltrate the area, all undetected. We were usually given targets that were five hundred to a thousand yards from our drop-off point. At the site of the target was a sniper instructor who had binoculars and a powerful wide-lens spotting scope for combing the countryside with his keen eyes, trying to spot a student on the stalk. Although we crawled on our bellies in Ghuille suits, it was difficult to remain undetected by the instructors. If we were detected before making our shot at the target, we were disqualified and possibly disenrolled from the course. In the July heat, crawling for hours in a heavy burlap suit was potentially dangerous, as heat exhaustion and fatigue were constant enemies. We had to learn to mask our movement by using terrain features such as gullies, high grass, bushes, and trees. The extreme factors involved in stalking made it one of the toughest exercises in sniper training.

The most stressful test for me occurred on the shooting range. Rigorous standards were set for passing grades on targets located up to six hundred yards away. Two different tests called "snaps" and "movers" were among the most difficult. "Snaps" were engaged from 200, 300, and 400 yards. These targets consisted of a small outline of a man's head and shoulders, which popped up behind the target line to be exposed for only a few seconds, and then vanished behind the dirt mound. The target could appear anywhere in a range of twenty yards. Between the time the target appeared and vanished, we were required to locate, acquire, take aim, and fire a kill shot on the target.

"Movers" were slim, man-sized targets that were exposed the whole time. These targets were difficult to hit, however, because they moved from left to right, across a range of twenty yards, at variable speeds—slow walker, walker, and fast walker. In yet another test, we had to engage and score a kill on a target that made a twenty-yard perpendicular or "full-value" movement, at varying distances, to a maximum of six hundred yards. This type of shooting called for nerves of steel and ice-cold accuracy. Bruce and I passed the test and were both in the top 10 percent of the class in our shooting scores.

We learned more about shooting than we had ever thought possible. Urban sniping, shooting through glass, and designing custom bullets for penetrating tough surfaces were some of the special skills we acquired. Techniques were demonstrated for penetrating electronic defense systems and motion detectors, as well as learning how to calculate, estimate, and prioritize distances of potential targets.

Our last test was the two-day Final Training Exercise. Bruce and I were partners, and in our mission we parachuted from a helicopter and infiltrated—via stalk—to a location that was two hundred yards from our target building. At that point, we dug an underground sniper hide, which was completely camouflaged except for two small loop-holes. Through those holes we were able to observe the activity at the target. The task was to document a killing shot on a certain man who was to appear for a brief time on the building. After documenting the shot, we exfiltrated for the last time. We had now successfully completed SOTIC, the Army Special Forces' only Category One sniper school. Completion of a Category One school meant that we were not only qualified Army snipers, but also qualified sniper instructors.

Little did we know, at that time, just how close we were to war. Our Army classmates invited us to join them for a SOTIC graduation party at the Green Beret Club at Fort Bragg. The highlight of the party was a hushed silence at the noisy club when a CNN special report on the big-screen TV flashed a scene of a United States Navy carrier battle group en route to the Persian Gulf. The anchorman explained that Sadam Hussein of Iraq had invaded Kuwait in a ruthless and sudden armored invasion on August 2, 1990. As Bruce and I boarded our flight back to San Diego to rejoin Foxtrot Platoon, I carried a fresh copy of Newsweek. During the flight, I read a story on the recent Iraqi invasion in which the commentator speculated what, if anything, the response of the United States would be. There was talk of American military deployment, and I wondered if SEALs would end up being deployed. But with some two thousand SEALs stationed around the world, and with many other platoons already in operation, I suspected that chances were slim that Foxtrot Platoon would be called on to deploy.

Bruce and I carpooled back to Coronado Island from Lindbergh Field to check in at Team Five. As we parked outside the Team compound, we could see through the chain-link fence that eight aircraft pallets were loaded with operational gear. Those pallets were used for airlifting the equipment of an entire platoon to a forward staging area. One of the members of our platoon, Brad O'Neill, was coming out to his car. His words of greeting still ring in my ears: "Welcome back, guys! Pack your bags; we're going to the Middle East."

PART FOUR

COMBAT ACTION

11.

THE RACE TO DESERT SHIELD

Foxtrot and Alpha Platoons, both from SEAL Team Five, were only a few weeks away from their scheduled deployment to the Western Pacific. We were the first two SEAL platoons to be sent to the Middle East and were selected because of our state of readiness. Our platoons were ready to deploy to Saudi Arabia as soon as the official word was sent from the SEAL admiral at the Naval Special War-fare Command in Coronado.

In the few days before leaving San Diego for the Middle East, Bruce and I were instructed to drive to the SEAL training camp at Niland, California, to "sight in" our two sniper rifles. The proper setting of telescopic optics on the weapons was crucial to accuracy. Bruce and I were both issued .50-caliber McMillan (long range) and .308-caliber McMillan (medium range) sniper rifles. After hurriedly packing our gear, we loaded a four-wheel-drive government truck and made quick time to the desert to carry out the critical sightings.

Amid scorching August heat in California's Imperial Valley desert, we had one day to sight in all four rifles. The conditions in the desert were perfect for our task. The dry, hot low-altitude of Niland was a close environmental match to the Saudi Arabian climate where we would soon be operating. This was important since bullets perform differently in diverse regions. If we conducted the weapons sight-in at higher mountain elevations, and then used those adjustments to make a shot at low-desert elevations, the result would probably be a miss. After firing many rounds through each weapon, we eventually adjusted our sights to hit targets ranging from a hundred to two thousand *(A MILE)* yards away. The .50-caliber McMillan generates a tremendous amount of overpressure when fired. The persistent thump of the large sniper rifle gave us throbbing headaches by the end of the day. Packing up the truck, we rushed back to San Diego to prepare for our flight out of Naval Air Station North Island. Swallowing Tylenol with a large cup of coffee helped ease the headache as we raced west on Interstate 8 toward San Diego.

The rest of Foxtrot and Alpha Platoons were prepared to leave, and we were told that our departure would take place on August 10, 1990. After receiving numerous briefs and gear inspections, we were given final orders as we were preparing to leave North Island. It was thought that Hussein's forces might have launched into Saudi Arabia by the time we were due to arrive, and both platoons were told that fighting might occur after landing. Those last few hours at the North Island airstrip were reflective and nostalgic. I gazed out at the mammoth Air Force C-5 Galaxy cargo plane, thinking of what lay behind and possibly ahead. At that point, it seemed like a thousand years since Donald and I had pretended to be naval commandos on Harrod's Creek in Kentucky. The realization struck me that I was now on the nation's cutting edge and soon to be among the closest and only individuals between Iraqi tanks and a defenseless strip of Saudi desert. I prayed that God would deliver our nation and our platoon from a scenario that even dovish liberals called an "outrage" and "rape" on the part of Hussein. I knew that the United States was prepared militarily, but I also knew that deliverance and victory only and always come, ultimately, by the decree of the sovereign God.

Foxtrot Platoon left North Island for the long trip to the Middle East. We landed for refueling in Labrador, Canada, and continued on to Rhein-Main Air Base near Anchorage, Germany. During the flight from Germany to Dhahran, Saudi Arabia, our C-5 was escorted by Air Force fighters. We were some of the first American troops on Saudi soil in the defense that would become known as "Desert Shield." Other than Air Force controllers, most of the troops arriving at that time were members of the Army's 82d Airborne and Special Forces units.

Exiting the plane onto the Saudi runway, we were nearly knocked over by a wall of heat. The average, daily high temperature when we arrived was about 120 degrees. Acclimating to the intense heat was no small task, and the thought of fighting in the heat was unimaginable. Intelligence reports informed us to be constantly on the alert for a sudden Iraqi armored offensive. Those first couple weeks were extremely tense as we waited for Hussein to make a move and prayed that chemical weapons would not be employed. After our arrival, the Naval Special Warfare Task Group Central was quickly set up at Half Moon Bay, which is only a few miles from Dhahran. There we established a defensive perimeter around our camp. A chain-link fence, sandbagged machine-gun nests, and SEAL patrols were our only primary defenses.

The initial challenges were limitless. We endeavored to stay healthy and hydrated, a difficult task on a diet of Meals Ready-to-Eat and temperatures reaching into the 120-degree range. We also had to travel everywhere with chemical-weapons protective gear. Moving about in the heat of day in a chemical suit could quickly induce heat exhaustion and even heat stroke. Further complicating matters was the constant terrorist threat that inevitably accompanies American soldiers in many Muslim nations. Coordination between Army, Navy, and Air Force control elements caused numerous complications and misunderstandings. Plans for escape and evasion from an armored assault were the greatest concerns of all. At Half Moon Bay, we were approximately two hundred miles south of the Saudi-Kuwaiti border and the occupying Iraqi troops. That distance could be covered in a single day by Iraqi tanks running at full speed.

We had barely settled in when our platoon was tasked to run special reconnaissance missions along the Saudi-Kuwaiti border, near the town of Ras al Khafji. Foxtrot Platoon had received orders to conduct clandestine patrols for observing the Iraqi troop movement along the border. To remain unseen, we slept during the day in concealed areas and conducted only stationary observation. At night, however, we moved about the border area and patrolled westward and inland for several miles from the Persian Gulf. Farther west, Army Special Forces conducted patrols in coordination with our platoon.

Conducting recon border patrols during the early days of Desert Shield was stressful. Our platoon was divided in half, with one squad back at Half Moon Bay, while the other squad embarked on the recons. Since we were required to conduct continuous twenty-four-hour watches, our squad was divided into two separate "fire teams." While one fire team patrolled, the other rested approximately thirty miles southwest of the border, at the site of a Saudi Royal Army reserve camp. These camps were scattered throughout the Saudi desert, attempting to form a defensive line in case of an Iraqi advance. But this strategy on the part of the Saudis was inconsequential, since they lacked the necessary manpower, weaponry, and training to stop any kind of serious attack.

The Saudi camps were sites to behold. The security was loose, and the troops, mostly reservists, were understandably fearful. Our platoon quickly decided that, should the Iraqis make an offensive move toward us, we were not going to be anywhere near a Saudi unit. Brad O'Neill, the point man for the first squad, nicknamed the site "Camp Speed Bump." His reasoning was that, if the Iraqi T-72 tanks started rolling south, the entire Saudi defensive perimeter would be nothing more than a speed bump in slowing down the tanks. Brad's comment was funny at first, but began losing its inherent humor as we pondered its truth.

Our immediate plan of escape in the face of an Iraqi offensive was basically to make a sprint to the ocean, inflate our Zodiac rafts, and head out to sea to rendezvous with a United States warship. In the process of extracting, we planned to drive south along the coast to evade attackers. We chose a coastal escape route so that, if our path was cut off or the trucks' engines failed, we could make a run to the nearby coast, and then swim out into the Persian Gulf and radio for extraction. A secondary plan of evasion was to radio in plenty of close air support and a helicopter pickup. Armed with only squad weapons and a crate full of AT-4 antitank rockets, we were in no feasible way able to survive an engagement with tanks or heavy infantry.

The border recon patrols were successful. As far as we knew, the Iraqis never identified us or detected our presence. Alpha Platoon relieved us by taking over the patrols for a time, as we began to rotate the border-patrol duty between our platoons. While we drove south to the Task Group at Half Moon Bay, we saw massive convoys of United States military armor and weaponry being trucked north to the front of the American defensive lines. Awed by the countless miles of M-1 Abrams tanks that were being hauled north, I remember thinking that Saddam Hussein must have either lost his mind or been ignorant to engage the United States in an all-out war. The size and potential destructiveness of the American war machine was an awesome sight to behold.

When we were not on the border, we spent most of our time at Half Moon Bay maintaining our gear and attempting to stay ready to fight at a moment's notice. Part of our readiness involved training in chemical-warfare protection suits. A full suit prevents air from coming in or out, restricting all ventilation. In the sweltering desert heat, wearing the suits caused quick exhaustion and dehydration. After testing the suits, we concluded that a SEAL, fully suited and engaged in a firefight, would be able to endure the full heat for about thirty minutes before being overcome with heat exhaustion or stroke. Looking back on those early weeks of Desert Shield, I shudder to think of the severe grief that Hussein could have caused by launching a late-August offensive. However, God's providence prevailed in answering countless prayers from around the world in allowing a slow, steady buildup of allied troops and weaponry and a steadily slow decrease in temperature.

As Desert Shield became a round-the-clock operation and coalition forces continued to grow, two SEAL platoons from Team One were deployed to join us. By October, Naval Special Warfare Task Group Central had acquired four fully deployable SEAL platoons. In addition, we had numerous naval support personnel backing us up in various specialties such as medicine, radio electronics, legal affairs, mechanics, administration, and Special Boat Units (SBUs). The Task Group was now ready for war.

As the Thanksgiving holiday approached, the two SEAL Team Five platoons, Foxtrot and Alpha, were moved north to the Ras al Gar Saudi naval base. At that location we were on the Persian Gulf with a full-length pier and a storage facility for our gear. Ras al Gar provided a perfect setting for training in waterborne operations. Also on the premises of the base was a Marine Corps helicopter squadron. Much of our training picked up speed as the weather changed to fall-like temperatures. Fancy open-ocean racing boats called High-Speed Boats (HSBs) were brought in to serve as a rapidly deployable means to get in and out of a target on the Persian Gulf.

Our time at Ras al Gar consisted mostly of training and rehearsals for future missions. I also spent many hours reading through the entire Old Testament and writing letters to family and friends back in the States. In November 1990, I began to pick up on certain clues that led me to believe war was imminent. One of those clues occurred on Thanksgiving Day and made it the most memorable holiday of my life. A small group of us drove a Humvee across the desert to a Marine unit stationed in the middle of nowhere. President George Bush was to arrive there and speak as he toured throughout Saudi Arabia. Seeing the President of the United States in person was a moving experience, especially in time of war and so far from home. The privilege was one of the highlights of my military service. I remember looking at President Bush among the hundreds of desert-cammy-clad Marines, all of whom were cheering and clapping in approval of their commander in chief. A phrase in Proverbs 30:31 aptly characterized that scene: "a king when his army is with him."

A patriotic and moving spirit filled the air as we heard our president pour on the "apple pie" rhetoric. Also present were Barbara Bush, Speaker of the House Tom Foley, and Senator Bob Dole. I remember seeing the frantic Secret Servicemen wandering about in the midst of hundreds of M-16s and loaded side arms. It must have been a Secret Serviceman's worst nightmare. President Bush's comments led me to believe that war was on the horizon. Reassuring us that four months of eating MREs and sleeping in the sand weren't going to be for nothing, Bush said that Hussein would leave Kuwait one way or the other and that we (i.e., the troops) were part of the plan. As Bush uttered the words, a roar of cheers by anxious Marines filled the air. A melancholy feeling came over me that day as I realized we were most likely going to war.

Certain United Nations resolutions, which specified a deadline for Hussein to move his troops out of Kuwait, were rapidly approaching their final date of January 15, 1991. I couldn't help but wonder whether the journalistic pessimism was correct in estimating large numbers of allied casualties and a prolonged conventional war. The month of December was probably the most reflective month of my life. For one thing, I didn't know if I would ever spend another Christmas with my family, and that caused many memories to flood my mind. Also, the Naval Task Group commander, Captain Ray Smith, enforced a stand-down period to allow us to rest up and minimize the chances of an injury. The captain's order for a stand-down is like a coach's order for a no-pads football practice before the big game: both are intended to keep everyone healthy for the action.

The final preparations were underway for the full-scale offensive that was soon to be known as Desert Storm. Both SEAL

Team Five platoons were moved north to the Ras al Mishab Saudi naval facility, not far from the Kuwaiti border. There we set up Task Unit Mike. That was to be our final forward staging base for launching missions into enemy-occupied Kuwait. The month preceding the war seemed to drag on endlessly since we all anticipated intense fighting at any moment. With the January 15 deadline only a couple days away, we were told to be ready to deploy at a moment's notice and were to stay near our platoon at all times. The stage was now set for the most intense chapter of my life.

12

DESERT STORM

On January 17, 1991, United States warplanes began bombing Iraqi targets. In the early hours of that day, our platoon was notified that Operation Desert Storm was now underway. As the sun rose on the first morning of the air war, I noted how peaceful and calm it was at Ras al Mishab. There were no sounds of distant bombs, nor was there any excited military-troop movement—just a beautiful, chilly Saudi sunrise with a slight breeze. The mind-set among most of us was one of peaceful resolve. At last, after six months of waiting and training, we were going to begin removing the "Butcher of Baghdad" from Kuwait. Most of the American soldiers with whom I spoke were eager to get on with the war, liberate Kuwait, and go home to the country and families we all loved and missed.

THE BIBLICAL ETHICS OF WAR

As a Christian, one of the theological questions I was constantly asked while in the Gulf, and am still asked to this day, went something like this: "If you are a Christian, aren't you supposed to lay down your weapons and push for peace, turning the other cheek?" I was asked repeatedly how I could be a Christian and in good conscience also carry out my duties as a Navy SEAL, not one of the more passive roles in military service. It must be understood, however, that in warfare the role of a SEAL is not morally different from the role fare the role of a SEAL is not morally different from the role of an infantryman, a tank operator, or a fighter pilot. All are prepared to use deadly force to carry out their missions. In fact, bombers and tank operators probably have a greater potential than SEALs to inflict death and destruction on an enemy. But it's hard to convince people of that because of Hollywood's sensationalized portrayals of Special Forces.

Oftentimes questions about the Christian ethics of war are a bit naive and uninformed. I could write many pages about the moralization of war in light of biblical mandates for Christians since I have reflected on that subject for numerous hours. The subject can become complicated because of a myriad of scenarios that may arise in any given armed conflict. But on a straightforward biblical level, I dealt with the questions in a way that usually revealed the questioner's lack of theological and biblical understanding about the doctrine of war and the Christian's role in it.

My first counterquestion to an individual is to ask if he could first explain to me what Exodus 15:3 means when it states that the Lord is "a man of war (KJV)." Next I would ask if he would comment on the scene of Jesus Christ's second coming to earth, as Revelation 19:11 states that "He [Jesus] judges and wages war." According to biblical ethics, the Lord Himself is pictured as both a "man of war" and One who wages war. By those passages alone, one cannot equate war and making war with immorality, unless one makes the mistake of attributing immorality to God as well. As Saint Augustine concluded, the true question is whether a particular war is moral or just, because not all wars are. One must apply biblical doctrines on war to a particular set of circumstances to determine the justness of an armed conflict. Biblical parameters have to be applied to the causes and means of war. For example, a war could have a just cause, and yet certain individuals participating in the war might employ unjust means in carrying out the cause. By that point in the conversation most individuals realize that specific issues about the morality of a given war are important and that numerous factors must be considered before one is ready to render an accurate moral judgement. The book of Ecclesiastes says that there are proper times for various activities on earth: "a time for war, and a time for peace (Ecclesiastes 3:8)." But to simply say a Christian should never fight in any war is greatly reductionistic and biblically without support.

I would hasten to add that I hate the tragedy and killing that war brings. I believe in first trying to resolve conflict peaceably, if that is possible. It is unfortunate that television and Hollywood have glamorized war and violence in tragic and un-Christian ways. However, there are times when the conscience of certain rulers-Hussein, Hitler, and Pol Pot, for example-runs completely unchecked. In those kinds of tragic and sad cases, physical restraint involving the taking of human life is often the only means to prevent the murder and rape of even more human life.

I had to evaluate the legitimacy of the Gulf War on biblical grounds, and I concluded that Saddam Hussein was engaged in evil aggression and was violating the confines of biblical warrant and human decency. Simply reading the reports about his campaigns from Amnesty International will suffice in convincing most skeptics of his brutality and disregard for the sanctity of life. Thus, as a SEAL and a disciple of Jesus Christ, I had no struggle in carrying out missions in support of my country with uprightness of heart. In fact, my strength in battle came especially from reading Psalm 18:32-34: "God ... girds me with strength, and makes my way blameless… He makes my feet like the [deer's] feet, and sets me upon my high places. He trains my hands for battle, so that my arms can bend a bow of bronze." The Lord is my strength in battle. But I will always abhor the underlying sin involved in war, and I long for the eternal peace promised in God's ultimate kingdom.

MISSILE ATTACKS BY IRAQI TROOPS

Meanwhile, intelligence reports informed us that a massive bombing campaign had been launched against Iraq and occupied-Kuwait. The exact battle plan was not revealed at that time, but our platoon was briefed concerning the general strategy of Operation Desert Storm. The bombing sorties were designed to remove Iraqi air assets, communication lines, supply lines, and to greatly damage and demoralize the enemy's motivation. We were not told how long the bombing would last, but were informed that the Iraqis would receive heavy poundings with explosives for a number of weeks to come. Then, if they had not pulled out of Kuwait, a ground invasion would commence.

On the second evening of the air war, I was preparing to put an MRE ration into a microwave oven in the cramped barracks at Ras al Mishab. The entree was corned-beef hash, and I had determined that the only way I could bear to swallow the stuff was to heat it and then smother it in Tabasco sauce. After I set the microwave timer for two minutes, the ground shook violently as a missile exploded close to our barracks. Soon after, another explosion rocked the foundations, and then another came even louder. We instinctively hit the deck and began to crawl to our rooms to find our chemical-weapons gear and helmets. Again the building shook violently as yet another missile exploded. Lieutenant Deitz yelled for everyone to don their chemical gear, flack jackets, and helmets. Headquarters radioed to inform us that there were no enemy forces in the immediate vicinity. Rather, we were under attack by mobile-launch ballistic missiles, which had been fired at us by Iraqi troops from the border area. Time seemed to stand still as the missiles cratered out huge chunks of sand and earth, shaking the glass in the windows. I remember the feeling of utter helplessness apart from prayer, and believe me, I prayed. At that point, all of SEAL training and the best equipment in the world would have been completely useless if there had been a direct hit from one of the missiles.

Some ordnance, such as ballistic missiles and mortars, require the constant adjustment of the launch platform to hit a target. For example, if a missile goes too far, overshooting and missing the target, a crew will note the miss and calculate an adjusted shot, hoping to get closer on the next launch. Adjusting shot after shot is called "walking the rounds in." Ed Mountain, one of the funniest SEALs in our platoon's second squad, humorously yelled, "Did ya hear that? They're getting louder! They're just walkin' 'em in." In reality, the missiles were being fired too far away for the Iraqis to have any observers mark the misses and call for adjustments. But each explosion did seem louder, and although we all laughed at Ed's words, the logic of his statement wasn't funny at all. It seemed like such a helpless situation that all we could really do was laugh or cry. It was typical for the platoon to laugh and joke in times of great potential danger. I never understood the mind-set behind it, other than to assume that the laughter was some sort of escape. In any case, we were never hit directly by a missile, and by God's grace, chemical weapons were never employed against us.

The next day was a stunning sight to behold. Until that first missile attack, we laughed and poked fun at the poor infantry grunts who spent countless hours filling sandbags for bunkers. But the day after our first missile attack, I have never seen two SEAL platoons become more resourceful in obtaining bunker materials. One thing is certain concerning the SEAL work ethic: we were not going to do menial labor if there was any way to avoid it. Digging a hole large enough for a bunker that several platoons could occupy would have taken a couple days with shovels. But through bribes and ingenuity, we persuaded a Seabee backhoe operator to dig a humongous hole in about ten minutes. The platoons looked on and gave plenty of moral support to the heavy-equipment operator. In one day we had built a formidable bunker ready for any missile attack, short of surgical nuclear strikes.

Another precaution against missile attacks was the stationing of a SEAL Team One platoon near the border to watch for Iraqi missile launches that would be headed toward our location at Ras al Mishab. Lieutenant Vic Myers's platoon succeeded in locating several missile launches and radioed ahead to us in plenty of time so that we could take adequate precautions before the missiles approached our position. The warnings gave us time to don chemical-weapons suits and get into the bunker before any missiles actually hit. For several days, usually in the evening, we experienced incoming missiles, but we all felt much safer in the bunker. None of the missiles ever scored a direct hit or caused any injuries. After about one week, the attacks stopped permanently because United States warplanes had destroyed all the Iraqi launchers in our area. One morning a UH-1 Cobra gunship buzzed our barracks on its way to the border to destroy more Iraqi targets, and we all cheered as the chopper passed low overhead. The camaraderie of American troops in time of war was an incredible experience. Knowing that any one of us would lay down our lives for any fellow soldier produced deep feelings that went far beyond the unity of high school or college team sports.

RECON MISSIONS BY SEALs

The allied bombing campaign is what launched the heaviest use of SEAL platoons during Desert Storm. Desert Shield consisted mostly of training and strategic border reconnaissance, but did not involve our going behind Kuwaiti lines. During the war, however, our operations chiefly involved recons behind enemy lines. One of those recon missions involved scouting a beach where my platoon would later carry out a diversion operation to fake Iraqi troops into thinking that an amphibious landing was underway.

The transportation we used: Most of our operations required helicopters and open-ocean racing boats to transport us into enemy waters in the Persian Gulf. Air Force MH-53J Pave Low helicopters dropped us close to the water with our rubber Zodiac raiding craft. The helicopters were equipped with the very best electronic, communication, and navigation systems. They also possessed the best weapons systems for our special missions and were capable of dropping us in pitch-black conditions "on a dime." The helos were piloted by some of the Air Force's most competent and talented pilots, in whom we all had great confidence.

The High-Speed Boats (HSBs) were driven by trained crews and were equipped with state-of-the-art navigation and weapons systems. Each forty-foot "cigarette" boat was capable of transporting a deflated rubber raiding craft and its equipment in the bow. In the rear of the boats, one squad of eight SEALs could ride standing up shoulder to shoulder. The boats often jumped completely out of the water and caused severe jolts in rough sea conditions. Capable of speeds in excess of eighty miles per hour in calm conditions, the boats quickly transported us to launch points offshore. At the launch points, we would inflate the rubber raiding craft with carbon dioxide cylinders, mount the motors and gear, and then complete our infiltration into a given target area, which was usually an enemy beach. Helicopters and fast boats were the two main delivery platforms used by SEALs during Desert Storm. A few smaller SEAL detachments used modified dune buggies with mounted machine guns and other weaponry. The dune buggies, called FAVs (Fast Attack Vehicles), were primarily used for Scud-hunting and land recons.

The threats we faced: The single greatest threat for SEAL operations in the Gulf was the floating antiship mines that were laid early in the conflict by Iraqi troops. Those mines were small and difficult to detect in the water at night. In a direct hit, one mine was easily capable of destroying an HSB and everyone on board. Another obstacle to our missions was the massive oil slick created by Hussein in the Persian Gulf waters. The slick consisted of semitoxic sour crude oil and was over one mile wide at certain points. The oil slick was more cumbersome than dangerous during water-borne insertions using the Zodiac rafts. Thick and nearly a foot deep in some places, the oil would sometimes be sucked into our outboard motors' water-cooling system. That presented the danger of overheating our engines. In addition, when oil splashed over the sides of the rafts, our equipment became coated, making our gear and weapons difficult to manipulate. So the oil served more as a hindrance than a hazard. We did manage to cope with the situation and carry out our missions.

However, during one particular insertion to conduct a reconnaissance, the oil became potentially deadly. Our platoon was in two High-Speed Boats for the ride to the launch point. All our patrolling gear was fastened in the front of the boats. The seas were abnormally rough on this night, and we were being pounded silly as the boats leaped into the air and then crashed down on the water. The pounding jarred our teeth as the powerful boats slammed down into one big swell after another. At one point, we hit a wave that caused a smoke grenade, in the forward part of the boat with the gear, to be completely ripped from its holder. Since the pin was also knocked out, the grenade was activated. As the smoke poured out of the bow, the HSB came to a sudden halt. We were situated hundreds of yards into the oil slick. Mike Gray and I scurried to the bow of the boat, attempting to locate the source of the smoke. At the time, we did not know what the source was, so we naturally assumed that the boat was on fire. Any flame could have ignited the oil, and we would have most likely all been killed had the oil slick caught fire. We dug frantically through the gear and eventually found the smoke grenade, which was now completely burnt out. After securing the gear, we continued on the mission. In the tense moments before finding the grenade, we all feared that, at any second, the boat might burst into flames.

On numerous different missions we experienced various other close calls. Iraqi mines were free floating, partially submerged, and difficult to see at night. Their tops barely broke the ocean surface as they bobbed along, carried by the currents. If a boat made contact with a mine, the explosion would be immediate and powerful. A mine was capable of vaporizing an HSB, and we spotted over a dozen of these floating mines while conducting missions. Once a mine was spotted, the general procedure was to note its location with the Global Positioning System (GPS) and record the data for intelligence.

During a reconnaissance mission, our Zodiac raft nearly struck a mine head-on at full speed. One of the persons in the raft saw something in front of us and yelled for the boat driver to swerve to the right. We had come only a few feet from being blasted into eternity. After circling back and marking the position, we all resolved to look ahead as intently as possible for other such mines. Having missed the mine, we adjusted our course and continued with the mission. The task was to send in swimmer scouts and recon a beach near Mina Saud. We slipped silently into the beach area in the heavy blackness of the early morning hours. No Iraqi soldiers detected us during the tense survey of the beachfront. After gathering the data we needed, we made our way back out into the dark Persian Gulf to rendezvous with the High-Speed Boats for our final exfiltration to the Ras al Mishab pier.

Those types of missions were typical of most Desert Storm SEAL assignments. However, the biggest SEAL operation during Desert Storm lay ahead. We had no idea at the time, but the low-scale recon of the Mina Saud beach would lead to the most successful mission of my career—a mission that would receive coverage on CNN and in Newsweek. Operation Michael Jordan would gain national attention as the highest profile SEAL mission of the Gulf War.

13.

OPERATION MICHAEL JORDAN

After more than a month of pounding Iraq by air strikes, the time had finally come to liberate Kuwait. In the course of warfare, the liberation of an occupied country nearly always consists of ground troops or infantry taking possession of the land. Although Hussein's forces were battered and impotent, they were still in Kuwait and were not with-drawing. Foxtrot Platoon was selected to pull off a major feint operation designed to lure Iraqi forces into believing that an amphibious landing was underway from the Persian Gulf. The occupied Kuwaiti beach of Mina Saud, which our platoon had scouted earlier during the air war, was the site for the diversion.

Our platoon knew little information about the specific operation until just a few days before its planned execution. Secrecy is always an important element of military strategy, and this operation was a pivotal part of the ground-war strategy. SEAL operations always strove for utmost secrecy because of the clandestine nature of their missions. Misinformation had been intentionally leaked to the press about a possible Marine invasion of the Kuwaiti coast, and articles appeared in major news magazines that predicted a maritime landing. Lieutenant Deitz did not brief our platoon about the specifics of the maneuver until we actually began to plan the operation.

The mission objective was to create the appearance of a

predawn reconnaissance and obstacle removal of a beach in preparation for an amphibious landing. To accomplish this objective, our plan was to plant six haversacks full of C-4 plastic explosives, which would be initiated by electric timers, on the Mina Saud beach. After swimming ashore to place the explosives, we would drop off large, inflatable, orange buoys, one on the right flank and the other on the left, about a hundred yards offshore. One-half hour before the explosives were set to detonate, our delivery platforms, the High-Speed Boats, would spray the beach with 7.62-millimeter and .50-caliber machine-gun fire along with 40-millimeter grenades. The whole operation was primarily designed to make lots of noise and to give the appearance of the initial stages of an amphibious landing.

The plan was to be carried out on February 23 and 24. All fifteen SEALs of Foxtrot Platoon would be transported in high-speed racing boats from the Ras al Mishab pier to within five miles of the Mina Saud beach. Located inside the bow of each boat was a deflated Zodiac raft, an engine, and gear for the mission, including the explosives. Once we approached Mina Saud, we would inflate and enter the rafts, and then make our way to the final swimmer drop-off point about five hundred yards from the beach. The final insertion leg of the mission was the clandestine approach of six swimmers to plant the explosives.

PREPARATION FOR THE MISSION

During mission planning we rehearsed numerous times by mock walk-throughs, as well as practice insertions and extractions with the boats. As part of the planning process, we engaged in a practice known to SEALs as "what-if-ing."

Everyone in the platoon is free to participate in this crucial aspect of mission planning where any and all possible contingencies are brainstormed. The only limits of what-if-ing were set by the individual's own imagination. "What if the outboard motor fails?" "What if we are compromised at points A, B, C, or D?" "What if our radio communications fail?" This process helps us to think ahead about every area that may jeopardize or contribute to the success of the mission at hand. Just as a chess player identifies how the loss of a pawn could affect the outcome of a match, so what-if-ing attemps to identify even the smallest problem that could affect the overall outcome of a mission. This method also aided in our planning for all the gear and weapons that were essential for operational success. During the days and hours before the mission we talked nonstop about the operation. Everything else in life took a back seat during those brief preparatory days. We were restricted from discussing the plan, both before and after its execution, even among other SEAL platoons with whom we shared living quarters.

The day for the operation came at last. On the morning of February 23, final preparations of the explosives were carried out by attaching two battery-operated, limpet-mine timers to each twenty-pound satchel of C-4. Using two timers for each explosive bundle helped to ensure detonation of the charges if one of the timers was either faulty or damaged.

The final tools to be prepared and loaded were our weapons. The six swimmers would each take one explosive charge ashore. Some of the swimmers carried Heckler and Koch MP-5 nine-millimeter submachine guns, and other swimmers carried the CAR-15 with an attached M-203, 40-millimeter grenade launcher. All swimmers had pistols as well. The other nine SEALs, of whom I was one, were to remain in the rubber boats a few hundred yards from the swimmers. We would be prepared to engage the enemy soldiers on the beach in a firefight if the six swimmers were discovered during their approach. Three SEALs would remain in each of the three rafts, with one SEAL driving, one operating an M-60 machine gun, and one as a radio operator, ready to call in air strikes. I was an M-60 gunner stationed in Lieutenant Deitz's raft. Even with the M-60s, we were not prepared for a heavy engagement since our platoon was divided into three, small, hard-to-coordinate elements. Shooting the M-60s over the heads of the swimmers at enemy forces, while bouncing around in the raft, was extremely dangerous. The thought of such a scenario didn't sit well with any of us. Nonetheless, we were prepared and willing to lay down our lives instantly for one another. There was never any doubt about that.

On the morning of February 23, as is often the case on eventful days, time passed by quickly. Before I knew it, we were in the briefing room of Task Unit Mike with armed security outside the room. The brief, called the Patrol Leader's Order, was conducted by Lieutenant Deitz, who explained every segment of our mission, including infiltration, insertion, actions at the objective, extraction, and other contingencies. After Lieutenant Deitz gave the brief, one of the officers present, who was not in our platoon, asked a chilling question. He queried what our platoon intended to do to negotiate the floating mines in the Persian Gulf since we would be moving at high speeds for many miles across the water under pitch-black conditions. The question wasn't as bad as the answer. "Nothing!" said Lieutenant Deitz. He explained that we would be moving too fast to see or even take evasive actions from floating mines. Also, the mines were too small to be detected by the boat's surface radar. The sting in Deitz's answer came when he said that, if we did hit a mine, death would be quick and painless. At his comment, members of the platoon glanced around the room with somewhat nervous smiles. There were even a few chuckles and one sarcastic "Hoo-yah!" *WHY WASN'T THAT WHAT IF'D?*

Following the brief, we made some final preparations for departure, now only a couple hours away. Our equipment was ready, and there was nothing more to do except the mission itself. I took a short walk on the pier and downed about four cups of black coffee to help prepare for a long sleepless night. Prayer was the last and most important part of my own preparations. There was a rather peaceful confidence in my prayer because I had begun to mature a little during my first year and a half as a Christian. I had come to know about God's absolute control and providence in everything that happened. God had protected me already in countless dangerous situations where death seemed imminent.

I was even prepared for death, if that should happen. No longer was death a fearful and unwelcome specter, because I knew that my physical death was but a doorway to the presence of Jesus, my Savior. The thought of being in heaven with Jesus excited me, and does evermore. My prayer was that God would be with our platoon and that He would grant us protection, success, and wisdom. I concluded my prayer by asking for, above all else, His will to be done. It was hard to imagine that His will might include the loss of our lives, but it was entirely possible.

My prayer on the pier continues to give me appreciation for the strength displayed by Jesus in the Garden of Gethsemane before He went to the cross to die for my sins. He knew that it was God's will for Him to die and still He prayed, "Not My will, but Thine be done (Luke 22:42)." I was confident that our platoon would survive, and yet it was not easy to prayer-fully leave my life in God's hands if that meant my death would honor Him most. Jesus exemplified the ultimate prayer warrior as He lovingly laid down His life for the glory of the Father's name. Thinking of the cross gave me tremendous strength as our platoon boarded the boats for Kuwait.

EXECUTION OF THE MISSION

Just before we set out from the Ras al Mishab pier, Commander Tim Holden, of the Task Force, wished us well and gave us his full support and confidence. At that time, and unbeknown to the rest of us, he whispered to Lieutenant Deitz that the ground war of Desert Storm was going to be launched at 4:00 A.M. on February 24. Our platoon would be among the first United States troops on Kuwaiti soil to start the offensive. The deafening roar of the dual 454 Chevy big-block engines in the boats signaled our departure from the pier into the calm Persian Gulf. While riding on one of the fast boats during the infiltration, I was manning a 7.62-mil-limeter minigun. It was a multibarreled, electric, Gatling-style machine gun capable of spraying thousands of rounds per minute. Of all the places on the boat, I was most comfort-able behind that minigun.

We made fast time on the infiltration because the seas were calm. Nearing the Kuwaiti border, we came under heavy black clouds that were a result of intense bombing and oil-well fires set by the Iraqis. The darkness was thick under the clouds, and I worried that the boats running at full speed might collide because we were traveling in a tight wedge-shaped formation. Arriving at our launch point early relieved a measure of stress and provided us with extra time to inflate the rafts and attach the outboard motors. We could hear the thunderous sound of distant aerial bombs being dropped by allied war planes in Kuwait. Before leaving the speedboats behind, Deitz asked the men in charge of each of the other two rafts if they were ready. He saw two thumbs-up, and we began to make our way toward Mina Saud.

We traveled west about five miles from the drop-off point. For the final mile, as we approached Mina Saud, the rafts were throttled down to a much slower pace, and the beach got closer and closer. About five hundred yards from the beach, we cut the engines and dropped off the six swimmers. The three rafts stayed together so that if our swimmers ran into trouble on the beach, we could drive in to engage the hostiles. The swimmers all carried small SCUBA bottles of emergency air that would last for about three minutes of breathing underwater. If the swimmers took fire, they could submerge themselves and have enough air to swim out about 100 to 150 yards from the shore while those of us in the rafts put down machine-gun fire on the beach.

As the swimmers went ashore, they stopped at a shallow depth of only a couple feet of water. Scanning the beach visually, they planted the explosives and activated the timers. Because the tide was going out, the haversacks were left on the ocean floor in about one foot of water. By 1:00 A.M. the satchels would be on dry ground when they detonated. The swimmers kept their eyes on the beach constantly while placing the charges and initiating the countdown timers. The whole procedure was conducted unseen by Iraqi soldiers. In only a few minutes, all six swimmers were on their way back out to sea to rendezvous with the rafts.

Deitz, who was one of the swimmers, radioed to us in the

rafts, requesting pickup about three hundred yards from the beach. His signal to the rafts was a series of flashes from a small red light. The light was unidirectional so that it could be seen looking landward from the rafts. But should the troops on the beach happen to be looking seaward, they would not be able to detect the light. Once Deitz and the swimmers were identified by their coded series of red flashes, we slowly motored the rafts toward their position for the final pickup. They were recovered without having been spotted and were unharmed.

After we took the swimmers into the rafts, we all went to drop off the two, large, orange buoy markers. When the sun came up, the buoys would be hard to miss as one looked seaward, and hopefully, they would be mistaken as channel markers for amphibious craft. We dropped the left-flank buoy first and then sped north to drop the right-flank marker; both buoys were anchored to the ocean floor. Finally, turning seaward, we headed to our final destination offshore, where we rallied with the armed racing boats.

The High-Speed Boats were right on schedule. After deflating the Zodiacs, we secured the motors and remaining gear in the bow of the boats. All four of the high-performance craft drove toward the Mina Saud beach in formation. The boats felt powerful as the gentle roar of the souped-up engines thrust the armed racing craft ahead. With four mounted guns on each boat, I felt a measure of pity for anything on the shore that morning. At 12:30 A.M. the boats opened up ferociously on the beach, and a maelstrom of lead was delivered on Mina Saud. Thousands of rounds of bullets were thrown at the beach nonstop for several minutes. When the guns ceased, there was no return fire.

The boats turned back out to sea, and as we vacated the

area, numerous small charges of C-4 were dropped into the water to cause a series of loud thumps every two minutes. At 12:55 A.M. Deitz had all four boats come to a complete stop and shut down their engines. He had to get positive confirmation that our explosive charges were going to detonate on schedule. At precisely 1:00 A.M., we heard six distant thumps in near succession. They could only have been our haversacks. Lieutenant Deitz couldn't restrain his smile as the highest profile mission of his career climaxed perfectly as planned.

The motors cranked up, and the boats rapidly exfiltrated in a southeast direction. We made excellent time in the calm Gulf waters, crossing the border into Saudi Arabia and finally coming to the familiar Ras al Mishab pier. The mission debriefing was short since everything had been accomplished flawlessly. The next day, before lunchtime, Deitz received word that our feint had been rated a total success. Intelligence reported two Iraqi battalions moving to reinforce the Mina Saud beach against a landing that would never occur. We also received congratulations from our Task Force commander, Captain Ray Smith, who was the highest ranking SEAL on Saudi soil.

The strategic implications of our completed operation were relatively simple to understand. First, Iraq was put off-balance by deception, dividing her troops and resources into needless reinforcement of an empty beach. Second, her troops were more thinly distributed and unable to be of any use against the main armored attack. And third, as the Iraqi troops moved toward Mina Saud, they were extremely vulnerable to aircraft strikes because they were forced to forfeit more secure, dug-in, defensive positions.

Reflecting on the success of what God had allowed us to

accomplish, I have ever since nick-named that mission "Operation Michael Jordan" because its coordination, execution, and outcome were untouchable. The mission also serves as a classic example of a proper employment of guerrilla-style (unconventional) units such as SEALs. Special Forces don't usually win the wars as much as they serve to supplement main conventional units and aid in low-intensity conflicts. The greatest effect on the enemy by SEAL teams comes from their untouchable surgical strikes and mythological ferocity in the minds of the enemy. The mission at Mina Saud made headlines on CNN, ended up as a feature article in Newsweek, and is included in numerous books on special operations in the Gulf War.

Although I worked with the very best of the best in the United States military, I know that ultimately God gave our platoon the success. It was He who guided our boats through mined waters, and it was He who allowed the United States and allied forces to have unprecedented low casualty rates for the entire Gulf War. Estimates of Iraqi soldiers killed range from 25,000 to 100,000. By comparison, coalition forces altogether suffered 200 dead and 500 wounded, a staggering statistic. Most of the allied casualties were from noncombat accidents. The low casualty rate and outcome of the war were tremendous displays of God's grace for the allies. After our country prayed for seven months, God answered. I hope that we haven't forgotten, or will ever forget, God's deliverance of the United States and her allies in the Gulf War. He is worthy to be praised.

PART FIVE

SPIRITUAL HIGHLIGHTS

14

MOUNT PINATUBO AND TRUE FAITH

A hero's welcome awaited our platoon when we returned to Naval Air Station North Island on Coronado. After Kuwait had been liberated, priority for sending American troops home was determined on the basis of which troops had been in Saudi Arabia the longest. Our platoon, therefore, was among the first of the returning American troops. Getting off the airplane to be greeted by press cameras, families of servicemen, and military personnel in dress uniforms was quite a festive event. Experiencing such a warm welcome home, I tried to imagine the reception of scorn and mockery that Vietnam troops faced when returning home from Southeast Asia. I resolved right then to thank any Vietnam vet whom I would meet in future years for their service. Although I was born during the Tet Offensive and was too young to remember the Vietnam War, it hurts to hear stories of how American soldiers and sailors were ridiculed and mistreated just because they served in a war that was not politically correct. In some sense, I felt a bit guilty, considering the fan-fare for us as we returned from Desert Storm. It was quite gratifying, however, to be appreciated and thanked for our service.

There was some difficulty settling back into the routine at SEAL Team Five. The two Team Five platoons returning from Desert Storm, Foxtrot and Alpha, had been among the few SEALs chosen for deployment to the Gulf. Every SEAL I ever met wished he had been in one of our platoons. SEALs always want to be where the action is, and that desire is a kind of prerequisite for being a SEAL in the first place. In a real sense, it was hard for us to receive accolades, medals, and ribbons in front of our teammates, who were equally capable and desirous of the same accomplishments. Nevertheless, I was now a member of a new generation of SEALs wearing the Combat Action Ribbon. Those ribbons marked the bearer as combat hardened and had previously been seen almost exclusively on Vietnam-era SEALs. For over a decade (1974-1990), SEALs had not seen any major war or combat. But for my own career, the timing of Desert Storm was providential.

AN INSTRUCTOR AT THE TRAINING DEPARTMENT

Many times, career success is mostly due to being in the right place at the right time. Such was my case, and I know that God guided my every step and had planned my course all in advance. After returning from the Gulf, I had completed two platoons and had two years of operational experience, along with combat action behind enemy lines. My new assignment was to the Training Department at SEAL Team Five. In that department, a group of more experienced SEAL instructors trained the different platoons as they prepared for deployment overseas. I aided the cadre in various aspects of weapons and tactics training. Marksmanship and sniping were my specialties, along with training SEALs for airborne operations and special insertions.

Packing parachutes and teaching SEALs how to rig their gear for parachute drops were just some of the tasks I was involved in at my new job. Qualified as a jumpmaster, I gave briefings on parachute jumps, and also conducted helicopter rappelling classes. In addition, I taught others the rigging pro-

SPIRITUAL HIGHLIGHTS

cedures required for the parachute dropping of Zodiac rubber rafts into the ocean. The rafts, nicknamed "rubber ducks," are used on airborne missions for clandestine infiltration of coastal, port, or riverine targets. The military C-130 Hercules aircraft, flying about 1,500 to 2,000 feet above sea level, would lower her rear ramp, and the raft would then be rolled out the tail, with the parachute inflating after the raft's exit. Once the raft, which held most of the operational gear, had cleared the ramp, a squad of SEALs would follow the "duck" out and parachute into the ocean. As soon as the team had splashed down into the water, they would free themselves from the parachute harness and swim to the raft to prepare for the transit to the objective. These "rubber duck" operations were usually conducted after dark or at dusk. The preparation and rigging procedures for the operations were a huge undertaking, and it was my duty to train other SEALs to rig the gear properly and safely. Attention to detail in rigging was crucial since a mistake might damage expensive equipment or possibly cause the aircraft to crash.

Another responsibility I had as a SEAL trainer was to teach rappelling and extraction methods for airlifting teams of commandos out of dense jungles and heavily wooded and mountainous areas. I also gave instruction in fast-rope operations, which involved sliding down thick ropes that were suspended from a helicopter onto ships, rooftops, and oil platforms (see pages 101-103). Training in nearly every SEAL tactic possessed an element of danger, but operations involving aircraft were especially hazardous since they depended on a combination of factors that involved the pilot, aircrew, equipment, trainer, and SEAL intersquad cooperation.

One example of the danger in our training occurred during an airborne operation that resulted in tragedy—a tragedy that God ultimately used to open new doors for me to share my faith with others. Early in 1991, Golf Platoon was to conduct routine parachute operations near the United States-Mexico border. One group of jumpers included a few new SEALs who had little airborne experience. As a trainer in air operations, my duty involved briefing the small group of platoon members.

The jump brief included basic procedural instructions, aircraft safety information, and emergency actions. These briefs were especially important for new and inexperienced jumpers, but often the excitement of the jump and the rush to prepare equipment according to fast-paced time schedules caused the jump briefs to be more of a formality than a serious part of the jump. Aware of the tendency for anxious minds to wander during the brief, I made a special effort to emphasize safety points that I believed were often overlooked by inexperienced SEALs. If the safety points were overlooked, an accident could possibly occur.

One such safety item was the need for overall "jumper awareness." This term refers a state of alertness by the jumper for keeping a cautious eye on his surroundings and watching carefully for potential collision courses with other parachutists, as well as obstacles near the ground. Parachutes can be steered and guided away from most problems such as trees, power lines, and fences. Simply looking around and being cognizant of the location of other jumpers prevents most accidents. But with new jumpers the thrill and excitement often override the cautious awareness needed to avoid problems.

This particular jump was further complicated because combat equipment such as backpacks and weapons were being carried. Once a jumper is airborne, the equipment is lowered by a fifteen-foot drop line, which hangs beneath the person so that the gear hits the ground just before his feet touch down. New SEALs tended to get so focused on the equipment that they would lose their awareness of other jumpers around them. Three times during my briefing of the platoon I specifically reinforced the importance of jumper awareness, stressing the dangers involved in midair collisions and asking them questions about certain important aspects. So when the jump brief was concluded and the guys headed toward the airfield, I hoped that they had listened and taken to heart the points that I had stressed.

The platoon departed SEAL Team Five in the morning for the jump. I stayed at the Team compound because another jumpmaster was on board the plane to supervise the drop. Around lunchtime, we received a call from the jumpmaster, informing us of a serious accident involving two jumpers in a midair collision. Both jumpers had been admitted to Naval Medical Center, San Diego. Later that day I learned that one of them had been paralyzed because of severe spinal injuries from his extremely hard landing. The other individual had received minor injuries to his leg but was in relatively good condition. Both were new jumpers who had attended my brief. The cause of the accident was exactly what I had been so cautious to try to avoid.

While one jumper was attending to his combat equipment, he lost track of other jumpers and collided with a lower jumper. They then became entangled as they rapidly descended to the ground. The bottom parachute created a vacuum of air just above the canopy, which had the effect of "stealing" the higher parachute's air pressure, causing the higher parachute canopy to deflate. The higher jumper then came plummeting down to the ground from over one hundred feet above.

Crashing to the ground with an abrupt impact inflicted severe damage to him, severing his spinal cord.

I felt a tremendous weight of sadness for him. But the Lord granted me peace that I had done everything humanly possible in briefing the jumpers to avoid such an outcome. I visited the seriously injured jumper at the hospital, and his spirits were surprisingly high, considering the circumstances. The only action that seemed appropriate was to pray for him, so I did. I also gave him a Bible and encouraged him to read it. He was a top-notch young SEAL and a tremendous athlete with national-class swimming ability. But now he would be paralyzed and confined to a wheelchair for the rest of his life. He stood as an example to me of just how fast someone can go from youthful health to paralysis or even death. God also impressed on me that life was fragile, even for SEALs.

A Second Deployment to the Philippines

The tragic injury of the jumper opened a new chapter for me in the SEAL teams. His platoon was scheduled to deploy in about one month from the time of his accident. His vacancy necessitated prompt replacement by a SEAL who was also a qualified parachute rigger, since the injured jumper had been the primary rigger for Golf Platoon. Golf's current platoon chief was Mike Bailey. Mike had been my favorite instructor during BUDS, and now he was serving with Team Five. He had always been a hero to me both for his combat accomplishments of decoration in Vietnam and for his sincere and professional style as an instructor and SEAL (see pages 64-65). I had not worked with Mike outside of BUDS training, but I always possessed a high level of respect and admiration for him.

A few days after the jumper's parachuting injury, my immediate course in the SEAL teams changed abruptly. While I was walking across the Team Five area, Chief Bailey motioned me toward him and said that he had something to ask me. As is Mike's habit, he got directly to the point without any extra words. He asked me if I would consider filling the injured jumper's empty space in Golf Platoon and be ready to deploy with them in a matter of weeks. Because of my great respect for Mike, his invitation to me to serve in his platoon was an honor that I still cherish to this day. I didn't need any time to think over his question, for an opportunity to serve alongside Chief Bailey was a true blessing from the Lord. I told him that I would be honored to serve and would be ready to deploy as soon as they needed me. Mike talked to the platoon commander, and the next day I was officially part of Golf Platoon.

There was nothing like the action of an operational SEAL platoon. Being in a platoon was the most enjoyable aspect of SEAL teamwork, and now I was back where I was most content: as an operator. It was sheer joy to be working with and learning from Mike Bailey. His experience as a SEAL in Vietnam was invaluable, especially in jungle-warfare, ambush, and demolition (explosive) tactics. Working on a daily basis with him was a dream come true. One thing was certain: God's hand had beautifully placed me in this new platoon for at least two life-changing reasons, which would become evident in the near future.

Platoons were like families, containing many interrelations and small-group dynamics typical of a tight-knit unit of people who lived together in close quarters. Fitting in with a platoon that had been training together for the past year was not always easy. However, Mike and I became instant friends.

Although he was not a Christian, we had many of the same ideas about tactics, and we went about problem solving in a similar way. Another instant friend in Golf Platoon was Eric Hatter, a second class petty officer. Mike, Eric, and I became close friends over the next year, and through God's grace, they were to become more than friends.

As the date rapidly approached for our platoon to deploy for the Philippines, an amazing and earth-shattering event occurred near Subic Bay, our destination. On June 15, 1991, the volcano Mount Pinatubo unleashed her fury in a massive eruption on the island of Luzon. Millions of pounds of sandy volcanic ash smashed the Philippine jungles to the ground. Hundreds of people were killed by the volcano's fury. The disaster was one of epic proportions. Upon hearing the news in the United States, I was first concerned for my brothers and sisters in Christ at First Olongapo Fundamental Baptist Church. I wondered if any of them had been hurt or killed. Had the church building been crushed to the ground? Were the people hungry? How were Pastor Henry and his family doing? Those questions and many more came readily to mind.

Answers to my questions would not come for a couple weeks, when I could go to the church and see the situation for myself. But I began praying for the church family right away. My heart would remain heavy until I was able to confirm the well-being of the church members. News reports were dismal, as hundreds of Filipinos had already been killed by the volcano around the area of Olongapo City. The heaviest damage, however, occurred at Clark Air Base in Angeles City. Thoughts of what might have happened to the people at the church flooded my mind constantly, and I continued to pray for their safety.

Before I left the United States, our Bible-study group in

Coronado had taken up a collection to purchase Bibles for our brothers and sisters in the Philippines. The believers there had a difficult time acquiring quality and affordable Bibles. We bought enough Bibles to fill a chest, and they were packed in part of my allotted space for personal gear to be shipped overseas. I had little room to pack extra clothing and everyday utensils, but the joyful thought of the believers in Olongapo receiving the Bibles was well worth the sacrificed space. However, as the platoon's plane took off, heading for the Philippines, it looked at first like the Bibles and the platoon were not going to make it to their destination.

The Air Force C-141 Starlifter jet, loaded with our platoon and gear, took off from Naval Air Station North Island for the first leg of the trip to Hawaii. About an hour into the trip I had managed to drift off to sleep. Suddenly, a loud school-bell-type ringing filled the aircraft. Somewhat groggy and thinking that I might have been dreaming, I opened my eyes to a most frightening sight. The ceiling of the plane's fuselage was filling with smoke. Oxygen masks had dropped from the overhead console, and the flight crewmen were running around frantically. The plane was making a steep dive toward earth, and we could feel the pitch of the plane tilting earthward. The pilots were attempting to drop altitude to obtain an increased level of oxygen. But from our point of view in the back of the plane, it looked like we were going down, destined to smack straight into the water.

Lieutenant Green, the platoon commander, talked briefly with one of the crewmen to find out what was going on. He passed the word on to us that the pilots didn't know what was wrong, but they were attempting to fly back to Naval Air Station Miramar, home of the Navy's "Top Gun" school. (The school has since relocated.) The crew informed us that the

Top Gun runway had the best crash crews around because of the fancy fighter training that took place there. The implication of the crew's statement was anything but comforting. Less than an hour in duration, the flight back to the California coast seemed like the longest flight of my life. But we made it back to the airfield, and the landing was safe. A picture of the eventful touchdown appeared in The San Diego Union-Tribune the following day, as there were fire trucks, ambulances, and emergency vehicles lining the runway for our landing. It turned out that a hydraulic line had been leaking onto·one of the plane's heaters, causing smoke to fill the plane. Nothing caught fire, however, and we flew out the following day with only a twenty-four-hour delay.

Flying to Hawaii, Guam, and finally the Philippines, the plane arrived in a place completely torn apart. The volcano had ripped down almost all the green, lush, jungle leaves to form a base of white ash, which made the surrounding hills look like the surface of the moon. This was not the same place I had been two years earlier with Charlie Platoon. At least, it sure didn't look the same. The once thick jungles looked like bombed areas of Kuwaiti desert. As we unloaded our gear and traveled to the naval station at Subic Bay, my heart was even more heavy because I wanted to know the welfare of my brothers and sisters at the church in Olongapo. I wasn't ready for what I soon found.

A RETURN TO THE OLONGAPO CHURCH

When liberty had been granted to the platoon to travel off base, I went straight to the church. The walk down Magsaysay Street, the main thoroughfare stretching from the naval base into Olongapo, was discouraging because of the many buildings destroyed by collapsed roofs. The weight of volcanic ash, comparable to the weight of sand, was too much for the cheaply built rooftops to withstand. The heavy ash was also mixed with monsoonal rains, which multiplied the weight exponentially. Flat roofs were especially vulnerable to collapse. But a huge wave of relief swept over me as I came to the church building. Still standing, it appeared to have escaped even minor damage. Staring speechless at the building, I knew that the Lord had taken good care of His children. There had been no structural damage to the church or the parsonage where Pastor Henry and his family lived.

My heaviness was further relieved when I first saw Pastor Henry. He was smiling and over-flowing with joy, as always. I entered the parsonage and sat with his family, who expressed more concern for me and my well-being than for their own situation. Their love and concern in light of the circumstances convicted and challenged me, and still does today. The Filipino Christians always struck me as being more concerned with relationships than with external circumstances. Recounting what had happened in the recent weeks with the Mount Pinatubo eruption, Pastor Henry told me something I will never forget.

Bearing in mind that the Philippines is a poverty-stricken, third-world nation, I was ashamed of my own weak testimony when I heard Pastor Henry's story. He began by telling of the death and suffering caused by the volcano. Many persons were killed directly by the ash, and countless other lives were lost by extreme flooding that resulted from the ash and heavy monsoonal rains. The floods also caused numerous families to lose all their meager personal belongings, as well as their houses. Water and food were cut off from many outlying barrios, and people were starving with little or no transportation to areas of relief. I was heartbroken at the story Pastor Henry proceeded to tell.

Describing in detail the church's participation in the relief effort, Pastor Henry said that lack of food was the main difficulty in most flooded areas. Because roads were cut off from supplies, certain areas were isolated from the regular supply of food and water. So members from the church made their way in boats to the stranded and hungry people, carrying precious relief supplies such as donated clothes and small amounts of rice. The members involved in the relief effort were themselves well below the United States poverty line.

The scene was one of dismal despair with gray skies, frequent rains, crushed houses, and many people either missing or dead. Children stood in the rain crying, with no houses, no food, and in some cases, no parents. Pastor Henry then told me about a situation that moved me deeply. Believers from the church had gone to give aid in a flooded area with no food. Volcanic ash covered nearly everything. Because of the monsoonal rains, the ash had formed a hard-packed layer on the ground. The combination of rain and ash sealed the ground and kept the air from penetrating into the soil. The lack of air caused earth-dwelling grubs to surface so that they could breathe. Pastor Henry said that many children began collecting the grubs, easily tossing them into small buckets. The grubs were then taken home to be eaten and shared with the other families. Eating the grubs provided the people with sufficient food to avoid starving. I fought back tears as Pastor Henry looked at me, and out of a heart of gratitude and thankfulness, asked, "Isn't it wonderful how the Lord always provides for us?" All I could think about was my overabundant life in America and how plush my life was compared to these dear brothers and sisters in Christ. But all Pastor Henry could do was praise the Lord and continue to thank Him. When we prayed together, he even said, "I thank you, Lord, for all the ash." And he meant it.

The facilities and creature comforts at the Olongapo church were primitive by American standards. But the worship was as true, as Spirit-filled, and as warm as anywhere on earth. The room climate for worship services was usually hot and sticky. On rainy nights, the tin roof leaked in a couple places, and one had to listen carefully to hear Pastor Henry's voice above the thundering down-pours. Nearly every Sunday, the church's electricity would fail, leaving the worship service to be illuminated by candles placed on the pews. As I reflect on the times of worship at the little Olongapo church, fond memories flood my mind. In the midst of physical discomfort from heat, humidity, mosquitoes, and unfinished board pews, the soft sound of the congregation singing hymns by candlelight, in praise to the Lord Jesus, will ever serve as an example to me of true worship.

Our platoon was involved in the cleanup effort for the Philippine people as part of the United States Navy's aid to the country. We shoveled countless wheelbarrow loads of gray ash and even did light construction work. The deployment with Golf Platoon was more humanitarian than combative. We faced no heated military situations during the six-month deployment, but spent our time training and helping to restore the Subic Bay naval base to its pre-Pinatubo state of manicured tropical beauty. In the months after our arrival in the Philippines, one of the most exciting occurrences of my life took place, as God expanded His glorious kingdom in the hearts of men.

15

AMAZING GRACE

Jesus taught His disciples that individuals who are truly born-again and repentant enter the kingdom of heaven through a narrow gate. In Matthew 7:13-14 He says, "Enter by the narrow gate; for the gate is wide, and the way is broad that leads to destruction, and many are those who enter by it. For the gate is small, and the way is narrow that leads to life, and few are those who find it." In other words, Jesus was saying that a minority, not a majority, would be saved in the end. Today, we might picture His metaphor this way: Those who are true believers are like the number of persons who travel on a country lane, but those who are lost are like the number of persons who travel on a modern superfreeway. Jesus' teaching leaves one who believes the Bible to conclude that there will be only a relatively small number saved in light of the masses of human history.

Firm is my belief that the Bible is God's inspired and inerrant revelation to man. If I take the words of Jesus at face value, the issue of how many people will be saved is clear: not many. I had therefore foolishly, and somewhat subconsciously, assumed that it would be highly unlikely that any SEALs in proximity to me would be saved. After all, since few people are saved—and since SEALs are such a minuscule fraction of the larger population—it would be rare and unlikely for more SEALs to be saved. Even if some were saved, I reasoned to myself, they would most likely be located across the world from where I happened to be. My assumptions were based on my experiences of three years of harassment by other SEALs because of my faith in Jesus Christ.

The first year following my salvation, I was optimistic and excitedly shared my newfound faith with other SEALs, but quickly learned that there is a vast difference between a mind of faith and a mind of unbelief. That's because the Bible says, "A natural man [an unbeliever] does not accept the things of the Spirit of God; for they are foolishness to him, and he cannot understand them, because they are spiritually appraised (1 Corinthians 2:14)." The sin-darkened mind of an unbeliever cannot understand the spiritual truths of God's Word apart from His saving work in his life. Although it appeared statistically improbable to me that more SEALs would come to Christ, I continued to "contend earnestly for the faith (Jude 1:3)" and witness whenever I had opportunity. Then God taught me this important truth: I must never assume limits to what I think God might or might not do.

While in the Philippines with Golf Platoon, I shared a room in the barracks with two other SEALs. One was Eric Hatter. Mike Bailey lived in a separate chief-petty-officer barracks and had a room to himself. As I stated previously, I had become a good friend of both Eric and Mike during our deployment, and they became two of the closest SEAL friends I have ever had. Our friendship was solidified through many hours spent together over-seas, often in close quarters. Early on, Eric asked me many questions about my faith, and he also began reading passages of Scripture that I had suggested to him. Mike began asking a sparse question or two about the Bible, but seemed largely uninterested in my faith. God began to move in Mike's life, however, while we had lunch at the Navy base's Sampaguita Club.

As Mike and I ate lunch together, he told me of an extraordinary situation that occurred during a mission with his SEAL platoon in Vietnam. The outcome of the operation nearly cost Mike his life. A piece of ordnance called White Phosphorus, or "Willie Pete," which was designed to kill a number of persons at once, exploded only inches from him. He was thrust off his feet backwards through the air, then landed on his back, and became enveloped by an umbrella of burning white-phosphorus fragments. Mike said that he felt like the incident was occurring in slow-motion. With his camouflage fatigues literally smoking, he jumped to his feet and ran from underneath the descending particles of white phosphorus. He told of how other platoon members who were nearby stood in silent awe of what had just happened to him. He not only had survived, but also was virtually untouched. I was quite aware of the destructive capacities of a white-phosphorus grenade, which had an advertised casualty radius of about twenty-five yards. But Mike had been only inches from the grenade and walked away unscathed. As he finished recounting the incredible scene, I said that it was simply unbelievable. Mike agreed by saying, "Yeah, I sure was lucky that day."

I could not, in good faith, let his comment about luck go by without a biblical response. So I said to Mike that either there was luck guiding the events of life in some way, or there was no such thing as luck, but a sovereign God, who was in complete control of everything that happened, including his survival of an otherwise fatal explosion. I said that he needed to decide whether God existed and had a plan for his life, or whether luck was running the show. Our conversation died gently, and we returned to our barracks. The next time Mike and I were together, away from the rest of the platoon, he told me that he had bought a Bible at the Navy Exchange and asked me what I would suggest that he read. I pointed him to the gospels, and he began to read and ask questions like Eric. It was not long before Mike had embraced Jesus as Lord and Savior.

My encouragement over Mike's salvation only increased when Eric Hatter soon trusted Christ as well. Looking back, I see that God was teaching me several lessons. First, God's salvation is not limited by anything, not even the elite status of Navy SEALs. Second, He was the One doing the saving because I had no clue that Mike and Eric were anywhere near to embracing Christ, and I had not done anything differently from my past three years of witnessing to other SEALs who had rejected Christ. For both Mike and Eric to have embraced Christ only weeks apart from one another was staggering to me. Third, God is so gracious to use a sinner like me to be His witness in proclaiming the message of salvation to others.

Both of them displayed immediate evidence of changed lives. They gave up blatant sins nearly overnight. They also became hungry to read the Word of God and spent their spare time reading through the Scriptures. Eric was even baptized by Pastor Henry in the South China Sea. I had never before experienced anything as great as having God use my feeble testimony as part of His sovereign plan to save others in Christ.

Mike, Eric, and I began meeting once a week to have times of Bible study, prayer, and fellowship. We listened to cassette sermons of John MacArthur's preaching and continued to grow in the faith. The three of us formed a strong bond while in the Philippines. Apart from my wife and other family members, I have never been so close to other Christians as with Mike and Eric. There was nothing in life as great as seeing others receive the "new birth" in Jesus and then grow in the Christian faith.

An amazing change now started taking place in my life. My aspirations of being a great naval commando began to wane as I saw something far more important: investing my life into the lives of others for the sake of Jesus Christ. For me, there was nothing in life more worthy of my devotion than to participate in God's expanding and eternal kingdom. That devotion is my underlying motive for writing this book, and my hope is that God would be pleased to use the testimony of Mike, Eric, and me to help win at least one more person to Christ, our Lord. If you do not know Jesus Christ as your Lord and Savior, I plead with you to do what Mike and Eric did: pick up the Bible, read the gospels, and heed the words of Jesus, who said, "Follow Me!" (Matthew 9:9; cf. 16:24-26. In the appendix of this book, there is a brief explanation of how a person can receive Jesus as his Lord and Savior and have his sins forgiven.)

God is so gracious, not only to save people from their sins, but also to use His children as witnesses of His salvation. From the times of SEAL training in Coronado until now, Mike Bailey has been a hero to me. But to have him and Eric as brothers in Christ is a blessing beyond anything I could have ever imagined. I am so thankful that God graciously works beyond all human expectations in saving others and in building our faith. Through Mike and Eric's conversion to Christ, God continued to direct my path in life and gave me new desires for my future occupational pursuits. I will always treasure the memories of my adventures as a Navy SEAL, but the occupation that once brought so much excitement and elation began to fade in comparison to my desire to study God's Word and be used as a vessel for the purposes of His kingdom. The salvation of Mike and Eric was a high point in my years as a SEAL and in my life, and being used by God to give people the gospel of Jesus Christ continues to be one of the greatest joys for me in this life. God's grace truly is amazing.

16

FROM SEAL TEAM TO SEMINARY

Golf Platoon completed the six-month deployment in the Philippines and returned to Coronado for reassignment. We had seen no combat action during our tour in Southeast Asia; however, apart from my own salvation, the greatest events of my life had taken place, as Mike and Eric were saved by God's grace. Shortly after our return, God granted me an honor and privilege that I had not expected. The highest goals that I had set for myself as a SEAL were soon to be realized after my deployment with Golf Platoon.

REASSIGNED TO THE TRAINING DEPARTMENT

When the platoon disbanded, Mike and I were reassigned to the SEAL Team Five Training Department. I could perfectly understand why the SEAL commanders wanted Mike as an instructor, but it was a bit of a mystery why they selected me to serve on the cadre in training other platoons. I didn't have near the expertise or time in actual combat as Mike had, and I ended up asking for his advice on a daily basis. Serving at the Training Department was a tough job, in part, because instructors often had to evaluate fellow SEALs, who were also good friends, and the evaluation occasionally included assigning a pass or fail grade. An instructor's responsibilities also included the direction and oversight of dangerous training scenarios involving live-fire operations, explosives, parachuting, and underwater maneuvers. Helping to produce proficiency in close-quarters combat and ship-attack operations was a significant task. But along with the weight of responsibility, the assignment brought satisfaction and a sense of accomplishment.

While at the Training Department, Rick Toms and I were given orders to a special close-quarters combat course at Fort Bragg, North Carolina. Rick had previously served at SEAL Team One and had been in the Persian Gulf during Desert Storm. We were both sent to train with the Army's Special Forces to sharpen our instructional skills for special small-unit takedowns and close-quarters engagements. Rick and I were the first two Navy SEALs ever to attend the school, and we both felt a great amount of pressure to make a good name for the Navy, for the SEAL teams, and especially for Team Five. A couple years before, I had attended a sniper school run by the Green Berets at Fort Bragg (see page 121), and now I was returning to this same compound at Mott Lake. Rick and I learned a great deal about our areas of specialty and gained valuable insights for implementing new training techniques back at SEAL Team Five. The Special Forces were always impressive. Although there are many distinct differences between SEALs and Green Berets, they performed their job well and possessed tremendous knowledge of special weapons and tactics. The Green Berets treated us well, and we made some great friends through the experience.

The training at Fort Bragg aided our job of preparing SEALs to enter buildings and carry out different strike takedowns. Rick and I traveled frequently with various platoons to conduct readiness exercises at a variety of locations. For example, we trained for urban assaults at Fort Hood, Texas, and rehearsed oil-platform takedowns off the Southern

California coast. Our schedule was hectic, but we became proficient at training platoons in our specialized fields of operations. I learned skills in nearly every form of combat.

During this time at the Training Department, I met and began training with the world's finest hand-to-hand fighter, Rickson Gracie. I had seen videotapes of Rickson (pronounced hik-son) fighting numerous times in no-holds-barred matches in Brazil. Seeing his fights gave me an appreciation for his abilities, and I am now persuaded that he is the greatest no-rules street fighter in existence. After calling Rickson by phone, I was able to begin training privately with him every week. His techniques are revolutionary, and I incorporated them into some of the training scenarios at SEAL Team Five. One of Rickson's younger brothers, Royce, received fame in the pay-per-view sponsored Ultimate Fighting Championships. Royce (pronounced hoyce) took the martial-arts community by storm and quickly gained recognition in most all the major fighting magazines. Royce, by his own admission, is not near the fighter that Rickson is, but the effectiveness of the brothers' style, called Gracie Jiu Jitsu, has produced a paradigm shift for hand-to-hand combat in the 1990s. Rickson is nearing a fighting record of five hundred professional wins and no losses. My skill in fighting increased greatly while training with him.

Rickson also became a good friend. He taught me as much about character, loyalty, and humility as he did about fighting. He is one of the warmest and most gracious persons I have ever met, and his ability to fight is exceeded only by his integrity and genuineness as a friend. Words would fail my attempts to characterize the full, positive impact he has had on me. The contribution of his combat techniques to the SEALs has also been great. I count it one of God's great blessings that I was able to train with and befriend Rickson Gracie.

SELECTED FOR DEV GROUP

The height of my own accomplishments as a SEAL came just prior to a major change of direction for my life. Ever since entering BUDS training, I, along with most other SEALs, dreamed about being assigned to Naval Special Warfare Development Group, or "Dev Group" for short. Dev Group selects only a limited number of experienced SEALs per year to come and train for their outfit. Receiving orders to that unit is a mark of success for a SEAL career. It had been a dream of mine ever since I graduated from BUD/S. But I always figured that the chances of my being sent to Dev Group, like everyone else's, was slim.

In 1992, I interviewed for and received orders to Dev Group. I was urged to screen for the selection process by our team's executive officer. I was surprised that they picked me and began training round-the-clock for the new assignment. My enlistment was up in March 1993, and I was required to have a minimum two-year commitment to Dev Group prior to coming. That meant, if I accepted the orders, I was required to re-enlist for at least three more years. Deciding whether I should go was one of the hardest decisions of my life. Accepting the orders would mean that my life career would most likely be the SEALs because the re-enlistment would put me at ten years in the Navy and halfway to retirement.

The other SEALs at Team Five thought I was crazy when I informed them that I hadn't made up my mind about whether to accept the orders. This was the opportunity that most SEALs only dreamed of. But the most important factor to me was simply God's will. The struggle to determine His will, however, was anything but easy. I had a desire to enter the ministry, but I needed much more than desire to seriously consider full-time Christian service. The thought of studying God's Word and teaching people about Jesus Christ thrilled my heart, and seeing God work in the lives of Mike and Eric prompted me to consider full-time ministry as a pastor-teacher. Still, I was hesitant to think that God would consider me to preach His precious Word. The thought brought fear and trembling to my soul, as it still does today. I felt much more unworthy to preach and teach God's precious Word than to go to Dev Group.

I had an additional desire that was drawing me away from making the Navy a career. That was my longing to have a wife and family. Early in my enlistment I had decided not to get married as long as I was on active duty as a SEAL. Seeing the hardships of married life in the Teams shook me up and made a vivid impression on me. I saw many marriages fall apart and numerous conflicts arise while SEAL platoons were deployed overseas for six or more months at a time. I simply refused to put a wife whom I loved through that. Going to Dev Group would mean that I couldn't seriously entertain the idea of marriage for at least another three or four years. The thought of not having a family in the near future created sadness as I considered whether to accept orders to Dev Group.

Besides my desire to enter the ministry and have a family, I had a desire to receive an education. Every member of my immediate family had a college degree except me. Up until 1993, my greatest educational experiences had come through my travels to fifteen foreign countries while serving as a SEAL, but the desire to get a formal degree was strong. Law enforcement work for a federal agency intrigued me. Also attractive was the possibility of going to law school after college. With many options for further education, my one big decision was whether to remain a SEAL, or to get out of the Navy.

I prayed daily for God's direction. As time passed, I slowly began to lose the desire to be a SEAL. There is no objective explanation for my loss of enthusiasm, except to say that everything I had once lived for now faded next to my desire to study and teach God's Word. Also important to me was having a wife and family, and I knew that having a family was in direct harmony with entering the ministry. Other SEALs thought I was crazy when I told them that I was considering getting out of the Navy and possibly training to become a preacher. Turning down Dev Group meant that the opportunity would never come again. It was truly a once-in-a-lifetime chance. The more I sought God's will through prayer and counsel from other Christians, the more my desire to go to Dev Group waned. At one time in my life, serving on the most prestigious SEAL team in the world was my highest goal, but now God was changing my priorities and was leading me to a new lifestyle and career. I couldn't help but think of the lyrics to the hymn "Turn Your Eyes Upon Jesus." The words to that song describe what was happening in my life: "The things of earth will grow strangely dim in the light of His glory and grace (H. H. Lemmel, Turn Your Eyes Upon Jesus [Singspiration, Inc., 1922, renewed 1950])."

HONORABLY DISCHARGED FROM THE NAVY

In March 1993, I received an honorable discharge from the Navy. Leaving my comrades and SEAL team was sad, but I took with me a prosperous enlistment, excellent health, lasting friendships, and a lifetime of memories. In the midst of this bittersweet time, however, I longed to enter college and strive toward a new career path, which I hoped would ultimately lead to the ministry. In July 1993, I moved to Fort

Thomas, Kentucky, where my mother and father lived, to begin classes at Northern Kentucky University (NKU). While I was completing a bachelor of arts in history in three-and-a-half years, God's call to full-time Christian service was confirmed in 1995. Living at home again with my parents was a great time, as I had been away from them for so long. While I studied for my degree, we made up for lost time during my six years in the Navy.

After graduating from NKU in December 1996, I was accepted by and enrolled in The Master's Seminary in Los Angeles, California. Finally, I would be studying the Bible professionally and worshiping at Grace Community Church, where John MacArthur preaches every Sunday. After reading most of his many books and listening to hours of his preaching on cassette tapes while in the military, I would now be able to hear him preach every week in person and also study at the seminary where he is the president.

God's grace is written on every page of my testimony, and He has had a sovereign purpose for everything in my life, even at times when I had no idea what was next. He has blessed my family richly by giving me, Andrea, the greatest wife I could ever imagine. He has saved my entire immediate family, as well as Andrea's parents, and my sister's husband and his parents. The extent of God's grace is truly beyond measure and proves to me daily the truth of Lamentations 3:22-23: "The Lord's lovingkindnesses indeed never cease, for His compassions never fail. They are new every morning; great is Thy faithfulness."

As a Navy SEAL who lived apart from God, the ultimate issues of life did not make sense. The problem of pain, the existence of God, and the reality of death and the afterlife were matters too weighty for me to understand, let alone resolve. I realized that no matter how highly trained I was or what my qualifications were, life could end in an instant behind enemy lines, or even on the way to the supermarket. The toughest military training in the world did not take the fragility of life away; it only caused me to see it more clearly than ever. That's why I am thankful that God met me behind the enemy lines of sin and Satan to rescue and save me from eternal death. Now my life is secure in Christ, and I am ready to meet God when I die. What about you? Are you ready to meet God when you die? That is the most important question you can answer in this life.

APPENDIX

GOD'S PLAN OF SALVATION

God's Plan of Salvation

The testimony of God's grace in my life has been retold on the preceding pages. My own experience of redemption in Jesus Christ-based on the trustworthiness of the Bible, God's written revelation to mankind, is as real as any physical object. The visible changes that Christ has brought about in my life are most clearly seen by those who knew me before I was saved. To my father, mother, and sister, my Christian actions and words are a complete reversal from how I once lived and talked. They know me to be a different person now than before I was saved. Now I *desire* to please God by obeying His every desire. I know that my inner change is all a matter of His divine grace working in my life to make me more like Jesus Christ.

I have written the following section as a personal message to any reader who would like to know how he or she can have saving faith in Jesus. I simply want to present to you the basics of the gospel, challenge you to consider carefully the salvation message, and have you count the cost of being a follower of Christ. The following words, therefore, are the most important ones I have written, and I urge you to take them seriously. I recommend that you also read the gospel of John (John is the fourth book in the New Testament and immediately follows the book of Luke) and the book of Romans (Romans is two books past John and follows Acts). Those two books complement the salvation message presented in the following pages.

Understanding the Good News

Man is a sinner. When Christians use the term "gospel," they are simply referring to the "good news" of Jesus Christ. Now good news pre-supposes that there is also bad news. You will fail to grasp the good news of Jesus Christ unless you first understand the bad news, which deals with your relationship or standing with God. The truth about your relationship with God is revealed in the only trustworthy source that we have, God's Word, the Bible. What does the Bible say? It says that everyone is born a sinner through Adam's disobedience, and that everyone is a sinner by his own choice (Psalm 14:1-3; 51:5; Isaiah 64:6; Romans 5:12). A sin is any violation of what God requires or forbids. For example, to lie is a sin (Colossians 3:9). To harbor hate or ill will toward another human being is also sin (Matthew 5:22). Those are a couple out of countless ways in which people sin.

The Bible says this to sinners: "Your iniquities have made a separation between you and your God (Isaiah 59:2)." Man knows that God exists as his Creator, but willfully suppresses his knowledge of Him (Romans 1:18-21). Because man is a sinner, he cannot please God, no matter how hard he tries (Romans 3:10-18, 23). Every person, then, lives in bondage to sin for which he is both responsible and accountable to God (John 8:34; Hebrews 4:13).

God is holy. One of the attributes or qualities of God is holiness. Holiness means that God is completely righteous, pure, morally clean, and separated from sin. Since God is absolutely holy, He will not tolerate sin and will judge it with severe punishment (Joshua 24:19; Psalm 1:5). Perfect righteousness, or sinless perfection, is what God demands. Even one sin, by thought, word, or deed, violates His perfect standard of holiness (James 2:10). Failure to live a perfectly righteous life condemns a person to hell, a real place of unspeakable and everlasting torment (Matthew 13:41-42; 2 Thessalonians 1:9). Since all men sin, there is no way for anyone to earn accredited righteousness and escape hell (Romans 3:20; Galatians 2:16). It's hard to imagine how perfect and holy God really is. In fact, He is so holy that a person cannot even look at Him and survive.

Since God is absolutely holy, He is also perfectly just (Psalm 89:14; 97:2). That is, He is always and completely right in all His dealings with man (Deuteronomy 32:4; 2 Samuel 22:31). Since His law (i.e., His Word) is perfect (Psalm 19:7; Romans 7:12), He is just in judging man for violating His revealed law. Unlike human legal systems, His justice never allows a person to escape by "falling through the cracks" or getting off on a technicality. God administers justice with 100 percent accuracy since all the evidence of each person's guilt is plainly before Him (Psalm 33:13-15; Proverbs 15:3; Hebrews 4:13). So there are no legal loopholes with God's system of justice. Because He is holy, He will not tolerate sin; because He is just, He will punish the sinner for breaking His holy law.

Christ died for sinners. Now comes the good news. God is gracious and has made a way so that men do not have to suffer punishment in an everlasting hell. "God so loved the world, that He gave His only begotten Son, that whoever believes in Him should not perish, but have eternal life (John 3:16)." As the Son, Jesus is the eternal God, who took to Himself an additional nature, humanity, through the virgin birth (Matthew 1:21-23; John 1:1-3, 14; 5:18; 10:30; Philippians 2:6-7). Simply stated, God came to earth in human form, and His name is Jesus Christ. Since Jesus is God, He is totally sinless (Hebrews 4:15; 1 John 3:5). He is also the Creator of the universe (John 1:1-3). Everything that exists has been created by Him and falls under His ultimate control. He therefore has full authority and is Lord of all (Matthew 28:18; Revelation 17:14).

About two thousand years ago, Jesus came to earth so that He could die a horrible death on a cross to pay the penalty for sin (2 Corinthians 5:21). In doing so, a bridge of grace was provided between God and sinners. God's justice was satisfied by Jesus' death as a substitution for the penalty of sin. God was, and still is, fully satisfied with the work of His Son, Jesus, as a sacrifice for sin. Through Jesus' death on the cross, a way of forgiveness was provided so that men could be at peace with God and have their sins forgiven (Colossians 1:20). Jesus not only died on a cross, but also was raised from the dead. His resurrection proves that God has accepted Christ's work on the cross and guarantees a future resurrection life for all believers (1 Corinthians 15:20, 23). The good news is, therefore, that a sinner, by trusting in Jesus' sacrificial death on the cross, can receive forgiveness of all his sins and thereby receive eternal life (salvation). A person who has eternal life is living in a right relationship with God in this present life, and when he dies, will live forever with Jesus in heaven.

RECEIVING ETERNAL LIFE

Turn from your sin. No one can receive eternal life apart from repentance (Luke 13:3, 5; Acts 17:30). Repentance is simply an inward turning away from sin. A person who is repentant will have a change of mind about who he really is. He will see himself as a guilty, vile, and helpless sinner before a holy God. Consequently, he will have a sense of sorrow for committing sins against Him, seek His forgiveness and cleansing, and turn from practicing sin willfully to obeying God's Word consistently (Matthew 5:4; Luke 18:13).

Believe in Jesus. True repentance involves true belief in Jesus Christ as Lord. Repentance and belief (or faith) are like two sides of the same coin. Repentance is a sinner's turning from sin, whereas belief is a sinner's turning to Jesus (1 Thessalonians 1:9). To believe means to put one's trust in Jesus alone as Savior and Lord (Acts 16:31; Romans 10:9). Belief is not complicated, it only takes a childlike and humble faith in Jesus. But if one truly believes in Jesus, his life will surely be characterized by obedience to Him (John 14:15; 15:14). The believer will have a new desire to do what pleases Jesus and will no longer delight in sin. That does not mean once a believer is saved he will be completely sinless in this present life. But it does mean that there will be a new and ever increasing desire to obey Christ and not to sin.

Receive God's gift of grace. Having your sins forgiven and receiving eternal life are a matter of God's grace, which means He gives His salvation to repentant sinners as a free gift (Ephesians 2:8-9). There is nothing you can do to earn His precious gift of eternal life. If it were possible to earn, it would no longer be a gift. But eternal life is something you can hunger and thirst after, and receive, if you repent and believe. "Believe in the Lord Jesus, and you shall be saved (Acts 16:31)." "If you confess with your mouth Jesus as Lord, and believe in your heart that God raised Him from the dead, you shall be saved (Romans 10:9)." If that confes-sion is truly believed and you commit your life to Christ and follow Him as Lord, you'll begin a new life of living for God and dying to self. You will then be saved.

Count the cost. Jesus cautioned sinners to count the cost of following Him before believing in Him. He illustrated His concern this way: "What king, when he sets out to meet another king in battle, will not first sit down and take counsel whether he is strong enough with ten thousand men to encounter the one coming against him with twenty thousand? Or else, while the other is still far away, he sends a delegation and asks terms of peace. So therefore, no one of you can be My disciple who does not give up all his own possessions (Luke 14:31-33)."

In other words, Jesus was saying, "If you think you want to be My disciple, first consider the cost of following Me: I must be the top priority in your life, not your possessions or even your fam-ily. You must love me supremely above every-one and everything (cf. vv. 26-30)." Jesus knew the impor-tance of planning for battle, but He also knew it was even more important to plan for the battle-field of life. Eternal life and eternal death hang in the balance. *your*

Call on the Lord. Jesus gives this invitation and promise to sinners: "Come to Me, all who are weary and heavy-laden, and I will give you rest (Matthew 11:28)." Only Jesus can forgive your sins and replace the emptiness and hurt that sin brings. Since that is so, "seek the Lord while He may be found; call upon Him while He is near. Let the wicked forsake his way, and the unrighteous man his thoughts; and let him return to the Lord, and He will have compassion on him; and to our God, for He will abundantly pardon (Isaiah 55:6-7)." Will you repent of your sins and believe in Jesus as your Savior and Lord?

NAVY SEAL. SNIPER. POINT MAN

Steve Watkins, member of the elite covert commandos that worked behind enemy lines in the Gulf War, tells his remarkable story in such a way that the reader can't put it down. But the inside story is even more compelling as Steve records how he came to a saving knowledge of Jesus Christ in the midst of his military service. It's my privilege to know him and his devotion to Christ, and his faithfulness in ministry.

— JOHN MACARTHUR
PASTOR-TEACHER, GRACE COMMUNITY CHURCH

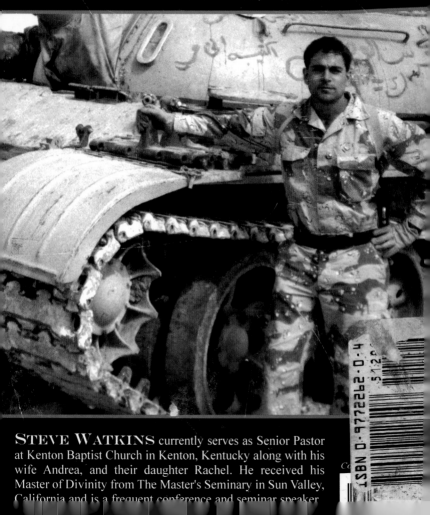

STEVE WATKINS currently serves as Senior Pastor at Kenton Baptist Church in Kenton, Kentucky along with his wife Andrea, and their daughter Rachel. He received his Master of Divinity from The Master's Seminary in Sun Valley, California and is a frequent conference and seminar speaker.

ISBN 0-9772262-0-4